Favorite Old Testament Passages

Books by DOUGLAS STUART
Published by The Westminster Press

*Favorite Old Testament Passages: A Popular
Commentary for Today*

*Old Testament Exegesis: A Primer for Students
and Pastors*
(Second Edition, Revised and Enlarged)

*Old Testament Exegesis: A Primer for Students
and Pastors*

Favorite
Old Testament
Passages

A Popular Commentary
for Today

Douglas Stuart

THE WESTMINSTER PRESS
PHILADELPHIA

Book design by Christine Schueler

First edition

Published by The Westminster Press®
Philadelphia, Pennsylvania

PRINTED IN THE UNITED STATES OF AMERICA
9 8 7 6 5 4 3 2 1

Library of Congress Cataloging in Publication Data

Stuart, Douglas K.
  Favorite Old Testament passages.

  1. Bible. O.T.—Criticism, interpretation, etc.
I. Title.
BS1171.2.S75 1985   221.6   85-5148
ISBN 0-664-24676-1 (pbk.)

Contents

Introduction

Many commentaries are, in actual practice, too complicated for most people to get much help from. That's a shame. There is so much useful information to be learned about the Bible from commentaries. But we are often kept from that knowledge by fear of having to wade through huge volumes written apparently more to impress other scholars than to help people who are eager to learn more about the Bible without becoming specialists.

So this book is different. It is basic and introductory. It concentrates only on well-known passages—from the Old Testament in this volume—and explains them for the reader's benefit in the clearest way possible. Perhaps it will help many people to see the value of consulting a commentary for their own use, and inspire them to read and study the Bible in a more careful, less haphazard way, picking and choosing wisely from the aids available.

We have chosen the Revised Standard Version of the Old Testament for the Bible text of this commentary simply because it is the most widely used version in English today. Whatever version you use, however—and we encourage you to consult others as often as you like—this book should still prove useful and easy to follow.

Both for simplicity and for thoroughness, the various passages are looked at from several different angles. A clarifying paraphrase, a brief introduction, notes on key vocabuiary words, an explanation of the passage's setting in the Bible, a description of its setting in history, observations on its form and structure, and some suggestions as to how its truths apply to us today are presented. This format helps us to see different aspects of the content, yet it also helps us to see the passage as a whole rather than merely in a verse-by-verse perspective.

For convenience of use, the passages are presented in the same order they occur in the Old Testament in our modern English Bible. This order is by subject. First come origins and law (Genesis–Deuteronomy), then history (Joshua–Esther), then poetry and wisdom (Job–Song of Solomon), then prophecy (Isaiah–Malachi). The passages come from all four groups, roughly according to the amount of biblical writing that falls into each category.

Chapter 1

GENESIS 1:1 to 2:4
The Creation Is Good

RSV	Paraphrase
1:1–5	Day 1: Earth is formless and empty at first, with water, but without light. God produces light, thus day and night. Naming of creation's parts begins.
6–8	Day 2: Firmament (atmosphere) is created. It holds atmospheric water.
9–13	Day 3: God causes land to appear, and from it plant life.
14–19	Day 4: God conjoins earth to sun and moon; atmosphere thins to allow stars to be seen.
20–23	Day 5: Sea life and bird life are made numerous and widespread.
24–31	Day 6: God makes man in heavenly image, with control over other species. Man is both male and female, and has food supply from plants and animals.
2:1–4a	Day 7: With creation established God rests. He blesses the seventh day as a rest day. The background story of the heavens and earth has been told.

Introduction

The Bible's first passage gives us an overview of God's creation of the physical world. People have always been intrigued by its seven-day structure and the evening–morning pattern of the days. More recently, with scientific theories about how the world developed and how life on earth began, the scientific reliability of the passage has sometimes been (needlessly) questioned. In the controversy, people often overlook how the passage emphasizes God's creative word, the goodness of his creation, his generous provisions for human beings—and all of creation—and the importance of adequate rest.

Vocabulary

1:1   *In the beginning God created . . .*   The Hebrew is better translated "God, in beginning, created . . ." or "When God began to create. . . ." The original does not imply that absolutely nothing existed or had happened before this. The separate creation of angels and other heavenly beings is already assumed (see v. 26).

heavens   The Hebrew term can also mean sky or heaven or even universe. Here it does not seem to mean heaven in the sense of God's abode, or the future home of believers, but sky; that is, what is out there when one looks up from the earth. Similarly in verse 8.

2   *without form and void*   Not at all in its present shape, but a barren mass of some sort, empty of life. This goes well with prevailing scientific theory that the earth congealed from a large mass of gases and dust.

the face of the deep   The surface of the watery mass.

	Spirit of God	The Hebrew word means either spirit or wind by itself, but in combination with God almost certainly means God's Spirit. Thus just as John 1:1 connects the Son of God with creation, this passage connects the Holy Spirit with creation.
5	*evening . . . morning*	The halves of the day as typically envisioned by ancient Israelites. See below, Form and Structure.
6	*firmament*	The Hebrew term refers to an expanse and comes from a Hebrew term meaning to beat flat, stretch, etc. It is not a technical term, but it indicates what the eye sees.
7	*waters . . . under the firmament . . . above the firmament*	Water on the earth's surface in lakes and oceans, etc., as compared to the atmospheric water from which rain condenses.
10	*Earth*	Also: land, territory, etc. On the importance of the naming process, see below, Form and Structure.
11	*each according to its kind*	This does not imply that there can be no crossbreeding, mutation of genes, or the like, but simply that fruits are predictable gifts from God, generation after generation.
14	*Lights*	The stars, the sun, and the moon. By these, in ancient times as well as modern, the seasons and the passage of time have been measured. Thus these lights are gifts to humans beyond just their aid in seeing.
16	*rule*	Dominate, be prominent.

20   *birds fly . . .*   Through the sky or across the sky, a
         across the   straightforward description of what
         firmament   one can see.

21   *sea monsters*   The Hebrew term refers to any large
                                 ocean creature, such as whales and
                                 the larger sharks, and need not be
                                 interpreted to suggest either
                                 mythological monsters or now-extinct
                                 giant creatures.

22   *Be fruitful*   Used with "and multiply," it refers to
                                 being fertile and reproducing in large
                                 enough numbers so that there can be
                                 animal life worldwide.

24   *creeping things*   These are insects, and also lizards and
                                 other small animals. Classifying
                                 animal life varies from person to
                                 person, and some of the ancient
                                 groupings were not the same as some
                                 of the modern ones.

25   *beasts*   What we usually call wild animals as
                                 opposed to domesticated ones.

26   *in our image*   The Hebrew could be translated "as
                                 our representation." The word
                                 "image" was routinely used in the
                                 Bible to connote statue or idol. Idols
                                 in ancient times were not, however,
                                 significant for their appearance.
                                 Ancient idolaters depicted their gods
                                 and goddesses sometimes as humans,
                                 sometimes as animals, and often in
                                 contradictory or crude ways. What
                                 the "image" actually looked like was
                                 fairly unimportant. "Likeness" in this
                                 verse does not refer to physical
                                 appearance. The image's importance
                                 was in its giving to the worshiper a
                                 sense that his or her god was present

through the image. The image/idol *represented* the god.

But the true God would not allow himself to be worshiped in this way. No idols were allowed (see Exodus 20:4–5). Rather, he put humans on the earth as his representatives. We are, as it were, his idols: not as worship devices but as envoys, servants, representatives to do his will.

The "our" indicates not the Trinity (God is always a trinity, yet never otherwise speaks in the plural to emphasize it) but angels and other members of the "heavenly host," already created.

27 *his own image*   There is no contradiction with "our image" in verse 26, since the heavenly host is also made in God's image.

male and female   Both are equally in God's image and both, according to the parallel language employed, are *Adam,* the Hebrew for humanity or humankind (RSV "man"). Thus distinctions of male and female are irrelevant when one is speaking of God or of how people are in his image.

29 *Behold*   The Hebrew term simply means look or see and is not intended to convey a specially dramatic announcement.

30 *breath of life*   The stress is on how plants and animals are different (animals have breath) and not on any special meaning such as eternal or spiritual life.

2:1	*host of them*	Their occupants or contents, especially the living things.
3	*hallowed*	Or: made it holy, set it apart as sacred to himself.
4	*generations*	An old term for background story, or lineage history. "Generations" is thus somewhat misleading in the RSV.

Biblical Context

This is the first creation story in the Bible, but it is hardly the only one. There are several others, whole or partial, and they each have a particular emphasis. For example, the creation story in Genesis 2:4 to 3:24 concentrates on human beings, especially the first pair, including their mutual rebellion against God and the awful effects of that. The brief little creation story in Genesis 5:1–2 is a summary of four features of the human part of creation: the likeness of God, the corresponding genders of humans, their blessing from God, and their being named (on naming, see below, Form and Structure). Creation is also the main theme of Psalm 89, with its stress on the fact that ancient Israel and its leadership represent a continuation of God's creation. Parts of Isaiah (e.g., Isaiah 40:21–31; 45:7–19) also recount, with emphasis on God's sovereignty, the essentials of the creation story. And John 1:1–5 describes the centrality of Christ, the Word of God, in creation.

Since God has chosen to tell about the creation in various places in the Bible, with various emphases, we should ask what is uniquely important about this account (Genesis 1:1 to 2:4). The answers in this case are found particularly in the form and structure of the passage.

Historical Setting

We really cannot date the events described here, since all of them go back before written history, and all of them together represent a great sweep of time and action. The only historical setting this passage can be given, then, is the obvious one: the very beginning of things, the first, vast stage of the world as we know it.

Form and Structure

The seven-day framework. Frameworks help make sense of details by organizing and associating them with one another. But frameworks also may convey a message of their own. Here, the word "day" in the framework cannot connote literal twenty-four-hour days, because the orbital linkage of earth and sun, necessary for this, does not even occur until the fourth day. (The old theory that the earth spun off from the sun is now obsolete. The proportions of chemical elements are too different. The current theory, that the earth and moon were captured into orbit around the sun, fits the biblical account much more closely.) The day pattern is part of an important message: Everybody needs to rest. Just as God took a day off, so should we.

In the passage, "good" is a prominent word. It is used so frequently that one can't miss the fact that what God did he was pleased with. Moreover, God blesses his creation (Genesis 1:22, 28), including the day that comes *after* he finishes (2:3). By this a good blessing—a beneficial protection—for humans is inaugurated, the "day of rest." Later (Exodus 20:8–11) this day is called the Sabbath, which means stoppage in Hebrew. The first creation story thus kills two birds with one stone. It gives us a sense of our cosmic roots, an idea of how things began, and at the same time teaches us that a frantic, seven-day workaholic pace is improper (something medicine now confirms).

We doubt that God needed to rest. But he did so anyway, as an example to us. In ancient times the Sabbath rule was essential particularly to prevent bosses or owners from working their employees or slaves day after day without rest. But a voluntary hectic pace in modern times is just as wrong. It is an anthropological truth that everyone needs rest.

The evening–morning pattern. In modern times, we begin our day in the middle of the night (12:00 midnight), a rather arbitrary arrangement. Some ancient peoples began their day with dawn, but many, including the Israelites, began it with sunset. They assumed, reasonably enough, that at sunset one day is ending, so another must be beginning. The first creation story is organized according to this pattern. Though the days of creation are obviously not literal twenty-four-hour days (see above), they are treated like days of the week for the purposes of suggesting the usual pattern of a week in which the days come and go until the holy rest day, the Sabbath, comes.

Note that on the seventh day there is no mention of the evening–morning pattern (Genesis 2:2–3). The seventh day is special, and the framework of the passage communicates this to us: Everything stops on the seventh day, even the repetition of the pattern.

The sixth day. It is no accident that humans and other mammals are created together. The Bible routinely groups humans and, for example, cattle this way (e.g., Job 1:3; Jonah 4:11). We *are* animals, but we are also *not merely* animals. Thus we are in God's image and are assigned dominion over the rest of creation, including our fellow animals (Genesis 1:27–28).

The naming process. In verse 5 God names (RSV "called") the light and darkness; in verse 8 he names heaven; in verse 10 he names earth and seas. Although any actual mention of the naming process stops here, the passage continues to name things, through to the end. Indeed, in the second creation story, Adam names the animals brought to him (2:19–20) and even Eve (2:23). Why this importance given to naming? Simply because what we name we know. Names give identification; they indicate understanding. God knows and understands his creation. But we may also know it and understand it in part, including understanding ourselves to some degree. In this way the naming process is one of the links between the first and second creation stories.

The colophon. The clause "These are the generations of . . ." in 2:4 is repeated ten other times in Genesis (5:1; 6:9; 10:1; 11:10; 11:27 [hereafter "generations" is usually rendered "descendants" in the RSV]; 25:12; 25:19; 36:1; 36:9; in 37:2 "generations" is rendered "history of the family" in the RSV). The most likely reason for this is that the brief sentences which begin "These are the generations of . . ." were titles indicating tablets or sections of tablets on which these stories were first written. Writing on paper was a rather late development in the ancient world. Before about 1000 B.C. virtually all writing was done either on stone (rarely) or on clay tablets. Tablets often had their subject matter indicated by a title line on one side, much as modern books have a title on the spine. The title line of a tablet is called a colophon. These colophons, reflecting the original tablet colophons, divide the book of Genesis neatly and helpfully. Genesis 2:4 is the first colophon, dividing the first creation story from the second (whose colophon is found at 5:1).

Application

1. We should remember that neither we nor the creation that we are part of is accidental. We came into being by the design of God, the creator of all that is.
2. God does not desire for us to lead hectic lives. Proper living involves proper resting. The need for regular rest is built into creation.
3. We are in part God's representatives on the earth, with dominion over it. This is a weighty responsibility, since it implies that we are to take care of the earth on his behalf and are not free to do anything we please with it.
4. Creation is still good. God has never pronounced it evil. We should receive it with thanks, enjoy it, and see in it evidence of God's constant provision for us and our fellow creatures.

Chapter 2

GENESIS 3
The Fall

RSV	Paraphrase
3:1–5	Satan in the form of a snake challenges the woman and the man to eat the fruit God has put off limits. He promises that this will make them as intelligent as God.
6–7	The two then eat some of the fruit, with the result that they become unduly preoccupied about themselves and their needs.
8–13	They try to hide from God, whom they now fear. They admit their sin, but each tries to place the blame on someone else.
14–15	God announces the snake's symbolic punishment: disharmony between humans and snakes.
16	God announces to the woman a punishment: pain in childbearing and conflict with her husband.
17–19	God announces to Adam a punishment: difficult work and mortality.
20–21	Adam names Eve. God generously clothes them both.

22–24   To the heavenly host God announces the expulsion of Adam and Eve from the garden for their sin.

Introduction

It would be hard to argue that the events described in Genesis 3 had no relevance to modern people. Our very identities, relationships, and patterns of behavior stem in part from our status of being in rebellion against God from the beginning of our existence as a human race.

Moreover, some of the selfish patterns of thinking that the chapter records are obviously still alive and well: the temptation to seek superior status, the tendency to blame others for our own faults, the attempt to hide ourselves from God when we do wrong, hoping he won't find out, and so on.

Vocabulary

3:1	*the serpent*	Not the first snake created, but snakes in general.
	subtle	Better: crafty, sneaky.
5	*your eyes will be opened*	You will be aware of things that you are not aware of now.
	good and evil	A way of saying: all sorts of things. See below, Form and Structure.
6	*a delight to the eyes*	Nice to look at.
	desired to make one wise	Looked to her like it would make them knowledgeable.
	of its fruit	Better: some of its fruit.
7	*naked*	Or: lacking clothing. The latter translation gives the needed sense that they were suddenly dissatisfied with things.
	aprons	Or: sashes, simple coverings around their bodies.

8	*sound*	Probably better: voice.
	walking in	Better: traveling through.
13	*beguiled*	Tricked, fooled.
15	*seed*	Offspring.
	he	The woman's offspring.
	bruise	Better: strike at.
19	*In the sweat of your face*	Only by working hard.
20	*Eve*	In the Hebrew this means Life.
	mother	Feminine ancestor.
23	*from which he was taken*	That he was made out of (cf. Genesis 2:7).
24	*cherubim*	Animal-like angelic beings.
	which turned every way	Swishing back and forth.

Biblical Context

"In Adam's fall we sinned all" says one sentence of an old children's catechism. The Fall was not a fall from perfection (perfect people wouldn't give in to temptation) but from guiltlessness. The first humans had no reason to be afraid of God, no disharmony with him, until they disobeyed a quite keepable rule: not to eat from one of many trees.

The story of the Fall is, then, one of temptation, sin, and punishment.

Temptation. Note that pride was a big factor in this temptation, as it is in so many temptations. Satan convinced them (the "you" in Genesis 3:1–5 is plural) of something that was only slightly true: eating from the tree of knowledge would make them like God. Actually, the fruit of that tree could do no such thing. All it did was to give them certain areas of knowledge they did not have before and were not ready to possess. Specifically, they became preoccupied with their nakedness and wanted clothing—something that they really didn't need and that added to their concerns rather than making life easier for them. This result of human sinfulness is still rampant. Humans have more knowledge than they are ready to handle properly, to which, for example, the arms race, economic exploitation, pornography, and any number of societal evils testify.

Sin. Sin is disobeying God. He sets the standards, and not meeting them is what sin is all about. But it is not as though the standards are impossibly hard; it is just that not meeting them looks desirable. To be selfish is usually more attractive than to be unselfish. To get ahead of others, to take advantage of them, to make yourself comfortable without regard for others—these things are usually more appealing than unselfish generosity. The lust for equal status with God, to know "everything" (including all sorts of needless and even harmful things) was the sin of the first humans in the garden. But whatever form disobedience may take in humans, the result is the same: estrangement from God, and punishment.

Punishment. Partly in reaction against some past overemphases on judgment and hell, many Christians have avoided any discussion of the idea that God would punish disobedience. We want our God to come across as always good and loving, and a punishing God doesn't seem to fit that picture. In fact, punishment is loving if it helps eliminate the sin that separates us, unlovingly, from God. And it is well known that without punishment in some form, the shaping of behavior is simply not successful (cf. Hebrews 12:5–11; Revelation 3:19). Moreover, God has graciously allowed us to escape the ultimate punishment, that of death (John 8:51).

Historical Setting

The Bible does not provide the sorts of minute chronological details that would allow us to date the time of the events described in Genesis 3. And there will probably never be any way to figure out scientifically the point at which God took the physical design of subhuman primates and remade it into true humans. At any rate, our passage takes place right after the first humans were made (Genesis 2). Most of the animals had been named, but Eve receives her name in this story (3:20). We are at the beginning of things, humanly speaking.

Form and Structure

The punishments in Genesis 3 come in the form of curses, which are verbal prescriptions for some kind of negative situation or condition.

The snake's curse (vs. 14–15) is really only symbolic. Whereas the humans and animals had all gotten along well in the garden before the Fall, now humans and animals would be in a situation of mutual distrust. The same thing could be said, of course, for countless animals other than the snake. The snake, as an animal, was innocent compared to the humans, who had a true freedom of choice and whose sin is the real focus of the chapter. The announcement in verse 14 that the snake would travel on its belly on the ground (eating dust, as it were) is not what would normally be thought of as a curse: snakes, we may be sure, don't mind that. And it was perhaps the way they were created anyway—the wording of verse 14 does not necessarily mean that a new mode of travel was being imposed on them. Rather, God called attention to the enmity between humans and animals produced in the Fall by calling attention to the slithering of the snake, something most humans don't naturally find attractive.

The curses progress to more serious conditions, including pain, domination (v. 16), the difficulty of survival (vs. 17–19) and, finally, mortality (v. 19). Death is the greatest of the punishments, the end result of sin (Romans 6:23).

In Genesis 3:5 the forbidden tree is called the tree of the knowledge of good and evil. Here, good and evil constitute a certain figure of speech called a merism. Merisms express totality by citing a polarity. For example, "Thou knowest when I sit down and when I rise up" (Psalm 139:2) means, Thou knowest *everything I do*. Or, "As far as the east is from the west, so far does he remove our transgressions from us" (Psalm 103:12) means, He *totally* removes our transgressions from us. In Genesis 3:5, "good and evil" means, all sorts of knowledge. It has virtually nothing to do with knowing the difference between right and wrong (which God certainly did not want to forbid). It instead indicates intellectual knowledge beyond human capacity to use it rightly. A major result of the Fall, then, is that we know more things than we can handle. We know how to hurt without knowing nearly enough about how to heal; how to rebel without knowing nearly enough about how to be obedient; how to indulge ourselves without knowing nearly enough about how to escape our addictions, etc.

Application

1. We all share in the results of the Fall. Part of the human situation is the condition of mortality.
2. Sin has its consequence: punishment.
3. Too much of the wrong kind of knowledge is not an advantage but a curse.

Chapter 3

EXODUS 15:1–21
The Song of Moses and Miriam

RSV	Paraphrase
15:1	Introduction: The song is a hymn of victory over chariot forces.
2–3	This rescue is God's doing, and God is Yahweh.
4–5	The Egyptian troops were defeated by drowning.
6–7	The victory is God's work. He is unbeatably powerful, destroying the enemy completely.
8–10	By a wind God parted the sea's waters. When the enemy was chasing the Israelites, God caused those waters to come in on them, while the Israelites walked on dry ground.
11–12	No god is like the Lord God, causing the enemy to die.
13–16	The Lord has brought his people to his holy place by might, and various nations in the area are terrified that what happened to the Egyptians could happen to them.
17–18	The Lord will settle his people in his land. Conclusion: The Lord is sovereign.

19 Prose summary of the destruction of the Egyptian troops by drowning.

20–21 Moses' sister Miriam and the Israelite women celebrate this deliverance with the same song, slightly modified.

Vocabulary

15:1	*the people of Israel*	Not necessarily all of them or all at one time.
	his rider	Especially: chariot rider. Pharaoh's army was organized around chariotry.
3	*the LORD is his name*	The Hebrew for the LORD is *Yahweh*, the proper name of God in the Old Testament (Exodus 3:14).
4	*host*	Army.
6	*right hand*	A term for strength. (Also in v. 12.)
7	*consumes*	Consume can mean burn in Hebrew.
	stubble	The dry, short stalk of grain left in the ground after harvesting, which burns like wildfire.
8	*heart of the sea*	Middle of the water.
9	*spoil*	What is captured and kept in war.
11	*terrible*	Terrifying. Not "bad."
12	*earth*	A common way of indicating the underworld, death.
13	*steadfast love*	Better: loyalty.
	holy abode	Either Mt. Sinai or the Promised Land of Canaan (or both).
14	*peoples*	Various nations and national groups.
	Philistia	The Philistine people who eventually settled on the Mediterranean coast of Palestine.

15	*Edom*	The people who settled in the country south of the Dead Sea.
	Moab	The people who later dominated the area east of the Dead Sea.
	Canaan	The various groups controlling the Promised Land.
16	*arm*	Another word for strength (see v. 6).
	pass by	Travel out of their territory.
17	*thy own mountain*	Better: the mountain country of thy inheritance. (Canaan is a mountainous country.)
20	*prophetess*	One who speaks God's word, representing him to his people.
	timbrel	Tambourine.
	all the women	An idiom for: women from among all the people of Israel.

Biblical Context

When Moses composed this song and Miriam popularized it, the Israelites were not yet in the Promised Land but still on their way to it. The song may have been composed almost immediately after the event at the Red Sea. On-the-spot composition was not difficult for expert poets. Moses was a prophet, as was Miriam, and prophets in ancient Israel were normally expert musical poets. Being a composer was virtually part of the job description.

Nearly all the prophetical books of the Old Testament (Isaiah, Jeremiah, etc.) are written mostly in poetry. Moses himself also composed the musical poems in Deuteronomy 32 and 33 as well as Psalm 90. Jonah composed the psalm of thanksgiving recorded in Jonah 2 while still inside the fish that had rescued him, not exactly under the best of conditions. So Moses and Miriam, on the move toward Mt. Sinai (where they will receive the Ten Commandments and much of the rest of the Law), could easily have composed this song, perhaps in a single evening. (Much documentation exists showing that modern folk poets in many cultures can compose elaborate musical poems without any rehearsal at all.)

So here is a hymn that looks back to a miraculous event fresh in the minds of all the Israelites, and yet looks forward to a promise of a land the people have not yet seen (Exodus 15:17). It is a song both of experience and of faith, of proof and yet of trust. Most of all it is a people's song, expressing praise to their God, Yahweh, the Lord, who was leading them—by displays of great power where necessary—every step of their journey.

For generations the only power most of these people had ever seen was Egyptian military and police power under the direction of the supposed god Pharaoh. Suddenly, they were seeing miracles performed by the God who was rescuing them from slavery to be his own special people. They had never seen anything like him before (vs. 11–12).

Historical Setting

On the basis of a date furnished us in 1 Kings 6:1, we can calculate that the exodus from Egypt, of which this psalm records the successful conclusion, took place about 1450 B.C. (A later date is also possible if the number in 1 Kings 6:1 is somehow symbolic rather than literal.) The event described, the drowning of the troops of the greatest military power of that day, took place at the Red Sea, the body of water between Egypt and the Sinai Peninsula. For a time it had been thought that the proper translation of certain Hebrew words in Exodus 15:4 should be Reed Sea, that is, a swampy area near the present Suez Canal route. But recent studies suggest that Red Sea has been right all along. The place where the miraculous parting of waters took place was probably somewhere in the north of the Red Sea, where it is close to the Mediterranean, but the exact location is not given in the Bible account.

Eventually, the Israelites would go to Mt. Sinai (chapter 19 and following) and then head for the Promised Land of Canaan (see Genesis 15:18–19). To get there, they would need to "pass by" (Exodus 15:16) hostile groups like the Moabites and Edomites mentioned in verses 14 and 15. But the song expresses confidence that they could make it, with God's help.

Notice that the song places a lot of emphasis on the name of God, the Lord (Yahweh, vs. 3, 11, 16–18, 21). One reason for this is that in those days, everyone except faithful Israelites believed in many gods, whom they called by many names. A lot of the Israelites were newly adopted into the nation (Exodus 12:38), and to them Yahweh was a new God. To almost all the Israelites, including Moses, the name Yahweh was new (Exodus 3:14). Here were people (like those in our day who become Christians as adults) for whom trusting in the Lord was a new experience. Thus they needed to be reminded of who it was who had rescued them from bondage and was leading them into a new life.

Since the hymn is in part a victory song, it is highly appropriate that Miriam led groups of women in singing it (Exodus 15:20–21). Women usually celebrated the victories of warriors (e.g., 1 Samuel 18:6–7). Here, God is the warrior (Exodus 15:3). No Israelite fighting men were involved. So the women's victory song is a hymn, a song of praise to God, not to men.

Form and Structure

The Song of Moses and Miriam is a hymn, which is a special category of song. A hymn is a song in which the sole emphasis is the praise of God for what he is and does. Typically, hymns in the Bible (most of which are in the book of Psalms) have three parts. First, they start with a brief introduction or summons to praise. In this hymn, the words "I will sing to the LORD" (Exodus 15:1) or, as Miriam modifies it, "Sing to the LORD" (v. 21), are the introduction. Next comes the bulk of the hymn, giving the various reasons to praise God, introduced here by the word "for." Psalms then end normally with a brief concluding statement. Here that statement is "The LORD will reign for ever and ever." Obviously most of the psalm is taken up with praise. Here the reasons for praise center on God's rescue of the Israelites from the Egyptians at the Red Sea. This event was a true miracle, showing God's power and protection over Israel to all the nations, including their potential enemies (vs. 14–16) in the area to which they were heading.

Some language in this psalm we must be careful not to take in the wrong way. The psalm contains an abundance of metaphors. A metaphor is a direct comparison without using a word such as "like" or "as." When the psalm says "The LORD is a man of war" (v. 3) it is really saying "The Lord is like a man who is a great warrior." When it says "Thy right hand . . . shatters the enemy" (v. 6) it is really saying "Your power defeats the enemy." When it says "At the blast of thy nostrils the waters piled up" (v. 8) it is really saying "The wind you caused to hold the water back was as easy for you to produce as for a man or animal to blast air out its nostrils." And so on. The hymn itself says it best, of course. The metaphors really pack a punch that nonmetaphorical language just doesn't. But we must understand what metaphors are, and not make the mistake of thinking that Moses or Miriam believed that God was a big giant with large arms and nostrils. That would be an insult to their intelligence, and a needless misreading of the psalm.

Application

1. God's greatness is seen both in what he is and in what he does.
2. Even the greatest human military power is nothing against God's sovereign might.
3. God deserves to be praised by his people for the faithfulness he shows them.

Chapter 4

EXODUS 19:16 to 20:20
The Ten Commandments

RSV   **Paraphrase**

19:16–20   Following the Lord's instructions, Moses brings the people of Israel to the foot of Mt. Sinai, where God appears dramatically in audible and visible signs.

19:21 to 20:1   God emphasizes to Moses that it is very important that the people realize that they can go no farther than the foot of the mountain. Moses and Aaron are the only ones who can go to the top. God then speaks what follows.

20:2   The Lord identifies himself as Israel's sovereign and rescuer.

3   Commandment 1: The Lord alone is to be God.

4–6   Commandment 2: You can neither make nor worship any idol. Continuing sin can bring more than one generation under God's judgment. Continuing righteousness, on the other hand, can result in God's blessing to countless generations.

7   Commandment 3: You should never undertake a pledge, promise, or testimony by an oath in the Lord's name that you do not intend to keep.

8–11   Commandment 4: Everyone must have one day a week off from work, following the example of God in creation.

12   Commandment 5: You must pay proper attention to your parents' needs if you want to keep the Promised Land.

13   Commandment 6: Do not murder anyone.

14   Commandment 7: Do not have sex with anyone married to anyone else, or with anyone other than your spouse.

15   Commandment 8: Do not take from anyone what is theirs, not yours.

16   Commandment 9: Do not lie when giving evidence about someone in a legal matter.

17   Commandment 10: Do not crave or desire to get something away from someone to whom it rightfully belongs.

18–20   It was so frightening to see and hear the manifestations of God that the people ask to deal only with Moses as a go-between, and not with God directly. Moses assures them that God does not want to harm them, just to cause them to take seriously their need to obey.

Introduction

The Ten Commandments are basic rules of behavior for a society that wishes to obey God. People cannot live together peaceably or justly without rules governing what they can and cannot do. These commandments are so foundational that they are even repeated in one way or another in the New Testament, as binding on Christians.

What they tell us about how God wants us to live has thus always been of great interest. If only everyone would *really* live by these commandments, what a different place our homes, our nations, the world would be.

Vocabulary

19:16	*third day*	The third day after the Israelites arrived at Mt. Sinai.
	trumpet blast	Horn sound; like a ram's horn, not like a modern trumpet.
21	*break through*	Cross the limit markers (see v. 23).
22	*consecrate themselves*	Prepare themselves to be ritually pure and worthy.
23	*charge*	Command.
24	*break out against*	Attack, harm.
20:2	*house of bondage*	The condition of slavery.
3	*before*	The Hebrew expression is somewhat ambiguous but probably means besides or except.
4	*graven image*	An idol.
	likeness	Image, worship object. The commandment does not prohibit art, etc., just the *worship* of any picture or sculpture.
5	*jealous*	The Hebrew indicates being on guard for what is right, not envious.
	visiting the iniquity	See below, Form and Structure.
	hate	See below, Form and Structure.
7	*take . . . in vain*	Falsely or fraudulently swear by God's name (Hebrew *Yahweh*).

9	*Six days*	Not more than six days.
10	*sojourner*	Resident alien.
	within your gates	In your town, community.
11	*hallowed it*	Made it holy; that is, special to God.
12	*Honor*	The Hebrew word is used in a special sense here: pay attention to the needs of.
16	*bear false witness*	Lie when giving evidence.
17	*covet*	Crave to get.
20	*prove*	Test.
	before your eyes	Always with you.

Biblical Context

The Ten Commandments are the first of over six hundred laws found in Exodus, Leviticus, Numbers, and Deuteronomy. The same ten are found also in Deuteronomy 6, where Moses repeats them for those who are about to enter the Promised Land, forty years after an earlier generation had first heard them at Mt. Sinai. So these ten are not the only commandments, though they are the most basic.

Their length, by the way, is not an indication of their importance. Five of the commandments are rather short, while five are rather long. But they are mixed together, quality being more important than quantity. Here is a comparison from Exodus 20:

Shorter Commandments	*Longer Commandments*
1 (v. 3)	2 (vs. 4–6)
6 (v. 13)	3 (v. 7)
7 (v. 14)	4 (vs. 8–11)
8 (v. 15)	5 (v. 12)
9 (v. 16)	10 (v. 17)

Commandments 2, 3, and 4 are the longest of all; Commandments 6, 7, and 8 the shortest. But this kind of unpredictable variation in length is just typical of the rest of the six hundred commandments and does not have an importance of its own.

In our passage, much is made of the fact that God made himself especially, vividly present when he gave his Law (Exodus 19:16–25; 20:18–20). This he did not to frighten people (v. 20) but to be sure they knew that *he* was the source of truth—not just human wisdom.

Historical Setting

The Israelites are at Mt. Sinai, at the southern part of the vast, barren Sinai Peninsula, just a couple of months (Exodus 19:1) after being miraculously rescued by God from their harsh life in Egypt. The time is about 1450 B.C. (see 1 Kings 6:1), and the laws the Israelites are beginning to receive are in many instances absolutely brand-new, without precedent in the ancient world. The command against idolatry (Exodus 20:4–5), for example, went against everything that all ancient religions practiced. Worshiping gods via their idols was central, normal, and routine in ancient times. For the Lord to ask his people not to do it was a big change, a leap forward in human knowledge of the truth that had no parallel.

And in a polytheistic world, where it was assumed that the various gods had their own specialties in running the world, a command to have only one God (v. 3) was equally novel. From the very beginning then, those who kept the Ten Commandments almost always found themselves at odds with prevailing, tolerated behavior. Indeed, is the situation really all that much different today?

Form and Structure

God's Law was a generous gift, making it possible for the Israelites to know what was expected of them. Imagine a boss hiring new employees, warning them that their jobs depended on strict obedience, then refusing to tell them what they were supposed to do! Knowing what was expected allowed the Israelites to know what was required for them to become and to remain God's people.

The Law was thus a covenant—a binding agreement between two parties, God being the superior party who *gave* the Law and Israel being the dependent party who *received* it. Israel's obligation in this agreement was to keep God's law. But God had an obligation too: to protect and benefit the Israelites if they obeyed or to punish them if they disobeyed. The Ten Commandments reflect Israel's basic obligation. God's obligation is mentioned in the promises of blessing (or warnings of judgment) found in places like Exodus 20:5–6, the end of verse 7, verse 11, and the end of verse 12.

Verses 5 and 6 are a key part of the obligation aspect of these laws. Verse 5 especially has often been misunderstood and therefore needs explanation. It looks as if it says that God punished innocent people for things that their parents, grandparents, or even great-grandparents did! The structure of these verses makes it clear that another interpretation is correct, however.

First, "visiting upon" does not refer here to punishment per se but to the *consequences* of sin. And those who "hate" God in covenant terminology are those who refuse to obey him; that is, sinners. Thus the verse says that sin which continues on and on, from generation to generation, is bound to have its consequences in each succeeding generation.

But then note the contrast in verse 6. Instead of just the "third and the fourth" generations of verse 5, we now read of "thousands" of generations of those who "love" (obey, in covenant terminology) God by keeping his commandments. In other words, while the sinful rebellion of one generation against God might cause a few subsequent generations to follow along and reap the consequences, God's real desire is an endless ("thousands") succession of generations knowing and enjoying his mercy and protection. The term translated "steadfast love" in verse 6 is actually better translated "loyalty."

Application

1. God's laws are gifts which are intended for our benefit, not arbitrary rules designed to make life hard.
2. God is their author (Exodus 20:2). He who created us (v. 11) knows best how we are to behave to fulfill the purposes of our creation.
3. God's laws are not to be taken lightly. Their author is, after all, also their enforcer (vs. 5–6, 7, 12, 19–20).

Chapter 5

JOSHUA 6
The Capture of Jericho

RSV	Paraphrase
6:1	Jericho is fortified against the coming Israelite attack.
2–5	God assures Joshua that the Israelites can capture Jericho if the soldiers will march around it daily for a week with trumpeting. In fact, the city wall will disintegrate before them when they shout on the seventh day.
6–14	The army follows directions and marches around Jericho daily with trumpeting but no other sound, the sacred Ark being part of the procession.
15–21	The seventh day, after marching seven times around Jericho, the Israelites gave the battle shout and captured the city, whose walls disintegrated before them. According to Joshua's order, they were allowed no plunder of any kind for themselves and could spare no one except Rahab and her family.
22–25	Rahab and her family were spared and joined the Israelites. Everything burnable in the city was then set on fire.

26–27   Joshua made the Israelites swear that none of them
would rebuild Jericho. God blessed Joshua, Israel's
leader. Word spread widely about him.

Introduction

This is an exciting story, and it is no wonder that Joshua 6 has
always been a favorite passage. It has drama, suspense, the tension
of battle, the excitement of victory, and the miraculous decomposi-
tion of Jericho's city wall to make it a memorable story. And it is
especially important as the fulfillment of a promise. God's pledge to
previously rootless Israel was that he was giving them a land. This
first great battle of the conquest of Canaan shows God's faithfulness
to his promise.

Vocabulary

6:1	*shut up*	Closed off and fortified.
2	*into your hand*	To your control or power.
	mighty men of valor	Better: soldiers.
4	*the ark*	The sacred box containing the Ten Commandments, etc. (see Deuteronomy 10:1–5).
5	*great shout*	A prearranged few words that everyone would cry in unison (cf. Judges 7:18).
6	*flat*	Not intact on its side. See below, Form and Structure.
	go up	Unto the city, which was up on a hill.
7	*pass on*	Walk ahead.
8	*ark of the covenant of the* Lord	The full name of the Ark.
11	*compass*	Circle around.

	camp	The area where the soldiers and people were encamped.
17	*devoted to the LORD for destruction*	See below, Historical Setting.
	in her house	In her family.
18	*devoted to destruction*	See below, Historical Setting.
19	*treasury of the LORD*	Materials to be used for the tabernacle/temple.
23	*kindred*	Relatives.
25	*dwelt in Israel*	Became an Israelite citizen.
	to this day	To the time when the book of Joshua was written, sometime after Joshua's death.
26	*laid an oath upon them*	Made them take an oath.

Biblical Context

Interestingly, one Israelite soldier did take spoils from Jericho after entering it, and with the aid of his family he hid those spoils under his tent (Joshua 7:20–21). His sin temporarily prevented the Israelites from making any further progress in the war of conquest (Joshua 7:1–9). Only after the offender was treated as the enemy and exterminated (Joshua 7:24–26) were the Israelites once again able to carry on with God's blessing.

In the book of Joshua, as elsewhere in the Old Testament, we note a very important theme: When Israel fights for God, God fights for Israel. That is, God doesn't just send the people off to do his will in battle; he actually does much of the fighting for them. That is how they were able to depart from Egypt against the wishes of a much more powerful army and its ruler (Exodus 1–15) or to march through hostile territory (e.g., Numbers 22–24) or to send puny, token troops against overwhelming enemy forces and still win (e.g., Judges 7). In the present story, God miraculously does the demolition work that leaves Jericho virtually defenseless against the Israelites. They are never on their own—he is always fighting for them, making up for their deficiencies, their inferiority.

Historical Setting

The capture of Jericho took place about 1400 B.C. not long after the Israelites had crossed the Jordan River and finally entered the Promised Land (Joshua 3). Jericho is just six miles from the Jordan River, on the edge of the Palestinian heartland, and thus a logical point at which to begin the invasion. But it was a great ancient city, founded around 6000 B.C. and protected by a massive high wall several yards thick, so thick in fact that houses could be constructed within its upper section, above the solid base (Joshua 2:15).

The invasion itself, including the battle for Jericho, was fought under a very special kind of warfare system called Holy War. Holy War was war commanded directly by God and was proper only for the taking and holding of the Promised Land. One of its purposes was the extermination of a genuinely wicked culture, that of the Canaanites (see Genesis 15:16), a culture which paid little attention to personal rights or morality and which exploited people for profit and power. Holy War could not be fought selfishly—for personal gain. Accordingly, the Israelite soldiers were not compensated but were all unpaid volunteers, and they were strictly forbidden to take anything for themselves from the spoils of war. That is one reason for the emphasis on the contents of the city being "devoted to the LORD for destruction" in Joshua 6:17 and 18. Indeed, one of the rules of Holy War was that if the Israelites would take anything for themselves that was "devoted"—that is, banned from personal ownership—*they* would become the enemy of the Lord, as the second part of verse 18 suggests.

Form and Structure

The passage is a straightforward historical narrative which, like numerous other passages, is centered on a battle account. It has a little poem near the end, Joshua's poetic warning (which by the way was fulfilled; see 1 Kings 16:34). Otherwise its structure is very simple: a challenge (Joshua 6:1–7), an obedient response (vs. 8–20), success (vs. 22–25), and a concluding warning and comment (vs. 26–27).

Especially noteworthy is the repeated emphasis on the wall falling down flat (vs. 5, 20). This does not mean a falling over intact on its side but a crumbling to the ground, so that the once formidable barrier was reduced to a simple insignificant mound of rubble over which the attacking troops could run into the city. Unfortunately, such a miraculous event would leave no archaeological trace, since there is no way to tell from the crumbled remains of a wall whether it disintegrated gradually or suddenly.

Application

1. God does not love war. The only legitimate wars in the Old Testament were Holy Wars, fought under very different rules and for very different purposes from modern wars.
2. God fought for Israel. He does not give to his people tasks too difficult for them and then abandon them to whatever happens. He makes his assignments possible.
3. God rewards faithfulness. He rewarded the Israelites for carrying out his very unusual seven-day battle strategy, and he rewarded a local Canaanite prostitute, Rahab, for her faithfulness as well.

Chapter 6

RUTH 1
Naomi and Ruth

RSV	Paraphrase
1:1–5	Naomi is widowed, and also bereft of her two sons, in a foreign land, Moab. The sons were married and therefore leave widows also.
6–13	The three widows set out for Bethlehem, Naomi's hometown in Judah. But Naomi urges her daughters-in-law to stay in their native land of Moab, where their opportunities for remarriage and therefore economic survival would be greater.
14–18	One daughter-in-law takes Naomi's advice but Ruth announces firmly that she wants to migrate to Judah with Naomi, staying with her and joining her people and her religion.
19–22	Their arrival at Bethlehem at harvesttime after Naomi had been a decade in Moab hardly goes unnoticed. Naomi expresses to all how greatly she has been hurt by the tragedy that befell her family.

Vocabulary

1:1	*judges*	These are the judges (governors, or leaders) in the book of Judges immediately preceding.
	the land	Israel, more specifically the part of north-central Judah where Bethlehem was located.
	to sojourn	To live as resident aliens.
	country of Moab	Not the country as nation but the countryside or farm country of Moab.
2	*Naomi*	The name means Sweetie in Hebrew. This will be important later (v. 20).
	Mahlon and Chilion	Both names mean something like Sickly One. Hebrew names were normally given at birth—not selected beforehand—to indicate birth circumstances or wishes (cf. Genesis 25:25–26). Naomi's sons may always have been frail, thus easy prey for the diseases that were fatal to them as young married men.
	Ephrathites	Natives of old Bethlehem. The oldest settlement there was called Ephrathah. It was later absorbed into the newer village called Bethlehem (cf. Genesis 35:19).
	Moab	The nation east of the Dead Sea and across the Jordan Valley from Israel and Judah.
6	*visited his people*	An idiom for: paid attention to or helped. It has nothing to do with travel on the part of God.
7	*on the way*	On the road.

8	*her mother's house*	Her family home. Women moved in with their husbands or their husband's families in ancient times, upon getting married (see v. 9). Orpah and Ruth had moved in with Naomi's family when they married into it.
	the dead	Their husbands and their father-in-law.
9	*lifted up their voices and wept*	Began to cry. In our culture we are not used to public crying, but it is very common in many cultures.
10	*Your people*	The Israelites.
12	*I have hope*	Of becoming pregnant. Naomi was apparently past childbearing age.
14	*kissed*	Kissed her good-bye. (In most cultures adults not married to one another are unlikely to kiss except upon meeting or parting.)
15	*her gods*	The Moabites worshiped a variety of gods, and individuals could choose among them to some extent. See below, Biblical Context.
16	*Entreat me not*	Don't ask me.
	lodge	Live.
17	*do so to me and more*	A standard way of saying, "May [the LORD] punish me . . ."
18	*no more*	That is, no more about Ruth's going back.
19	*the whole town*	An idiom for: people all over town.
	Is this Naomi?	An idiom equivalent to: Well, what do you know—it's Naomi!
20	*Mara*	Hebrew for bitter. The symbolic name change had significance. See below, Biblical Context.

	the Almighty	The Hebrew term means, literally, "the Mountain One," one of many terms for God in the Old Testament. Naomi is speaking almost poetically, here, and uses "the Almighty" in parallel to "the Lord."
21	*brought calamity upon me*	Or: caused me to have trouble, or the like.
22	*barley harvest*	So-called spring barley, the most common type in Bible times, was harvested in April–May. Indeed, Barley Harvest was the name for the ancient month that ran from mid-April to mid-May in Israel, as evidenced by the later Gezer Calendar.

Biblical Context

In our English Bibles, Ruth comes after Judges because its action takes place during that same era. The days of the Judges were characterized by frequent oppression of the Israelites by their enemies, including Moab (Judges 3:12–15), as a result of Israel's unfaithfulness to God (Judges 2:11–23).

The story of Ruth provides a local and individual contrast to what was generally happening in those days. Naomi, Ruth, and the people of Bethlehem show love for one another in an age of hostility and show love for the true God in an age of idolatry and unbelief.

Both Orpah and Ruth had grown up worshiping the Moabite gods (v. 15). Chief among these was Chemosh, the national god (Numbers 21:29; Judges 11:24; 1 Kings 11:7, 33). But the Moabites, like virtually all peoples except orthodox Israelites, worshiped many gods (that is, practiced polytheism) with the aid of many idols. When Ruth tells Naomi that "your God" will be "my God" she is making a decisive commitment to convert to Yahwism (belief in Yahweh), the true religion of Israel. This would mean abandoning idolatry and polytheism, which she had probably practiced in contrast to her in-laws (on a wife's religion being different from her husband's, cf. 1 Kings 11:4–8; Ezra 9:1–12; Malachi 2:11). Since in Bible times virtually everyone was religious, conversion was not so much a matter of turning from unbelief to belief as it was of choosing new gods (Judges 5:8), strange as this may sound to us. In modern times, our "false gods" tend to be material things or life-styles rather than deities per se (1 John 2:15–17; 5:19–21).

Naomi's proposal that her name should be changed to Mara (Bitter) in Ruth 1:20 is a way of declaring the severity of her tragedy. People understood, of course, that she didn't really intend that they would actually call her Mara: throughout the book she is still called Naomi. But name changes, actual or merely figurative as in this case, were very significant in ancient Israel. Names were carefully chosen to give an appropriateness to a person. They were not necessarily descriptive of character but were more important to self-identity than in our own day and culture. Thus when a new relationship to God had been established for him, Abram's name was changed, just slightly, to the similar Abraham (Genesis 17:5). Jacob's name was changed to Israel when his status changed (Genesis 32:28). By her tongue-in-cheek name change, Naomi says, in effect, "Things are different now. Because of what has happened, I'm not exactly the same person that I was."

Historical Setting

The Israelites entered the Promised Land of Canaan around 1400 B.C., if the dating in 1 Kings 6:1 is taken literally, or perhaps around 1225 B.C., if "480 years" is considered to be a way of expressing "twelve generations." Thereafter began the era of the Judges, which lasted until Saul became king about 1031 B.C. (1 Samuel 11). From the genealogy in Ruth 4:17–22 it is possible to work back to a time around 1100 B.C. for our story. As that genealogy reveals, by the way, Ruth was King David's great-grandmother. So our story is about a brave and loyal foreign woman whose offspring led to the royal dynasty and to Christ himself (Matthew 1:5–16).

Moab was a foreign country right on Judah's border whose language was virtually identical to Hebrew but whose religion was very different. Moreover, it was sometimes an enemy of the Israelites (Numbers 22–25; Joshua 24:9; Judges 3:12–30). But Naomi and her family had obviously found acceptance there, and Ruth, though a Moabite, found acceptance among Israelites in Bethlehem also (Ruth 2:11–12).

The trip from the countryside of Moab back to Bethlehem, by the way, need not have been a terribly long one. It could have been as short as forty miles, depending on where in Moab Naomi and her family had been living. Thus in a day or two they would be able to complete their journey. They would, of course, have known that it was barley-harvest time when they were arriving and that the wheat harvest would follow two to three weeks later. So Naomi chose a logical time for their trip, one in which their chances of survival, temporarily at least, would be higher.

Form and Structure

The passage is a historical narrative recounting the history of Naomi's misfortunes from the time she left Bethlehem to the time she returned. But an important element has been introduced into the tragic story: the person of Ruth. Naomi cannot possibly know it yet, but through Ruth will come a preservation of Naomi's family line (Ruth 4:5, 10) and even another "son" (4:17).

The overall progression of events is easy enough to follow and may be outlined as follows:

Ruth 1:1–5   Naomi's tragedy unfolds
    6–13   Her decision to return and its implications
  14–18   The contrasting reactions of her daughters-in-law
  19–22   Naomi's arrival in Bethlehem and reactions there

Note that women are the ones who initiate most of the decisive action in the story. Naomi decides to return to Bethlehem; Ruth determines to go with her. This pattern continues throughout the book. Ruth will initiate the gleaning of grain (2:2); Naomi will urge her to stay in Boaz's field (2:22), will initiate the proposal of marriage to Boaz (3:1–3), and will predict Boaz's reaction (3:4). Ruth then handles the proposal itself skillfully (3:6–8). Naomi even predicts Boaz's response in terms of the legal process necessary to marry Ruth and thus continue in effect the lineage of Naomi (3:18). It is the women of Bethlehem who identify the child of Ruth and Boaz as a true replacement for Naomi's dead sons (4:14–17) and Naomi who helps bring him up (4:16).

The story does not deny the responsible roles of men; Boaz shows himself clever and decisive too (2:8–12; 2:14–16; 3:11–13; 4:1–10). But it especially emphasizes the influence that godly women may have in shaping their own circumstances and in determining the best course of action in a given situation.

Naomi and Ruth are people who know how to be faithful to God even in personal tragedy. Naomi shows how deeply her tragedy has hurt her (vs. 13, 20) by emphasizing the bitterness of her situation, but she never fails to acknowledge God. Ruth converts to this God, Yahweh, though her own loss has also been great.

Application

1. True faith proves real not only in good times but especially in bad times, when from the human point of view there seems to be little hope (cf. Ruth 1:11).
2. One never can tell what good things may come in the future from acts of faithfulness done now. How could Ruth have known that she would one day be famed as the great-grandmother of Israel's greatest king?
3. Conversion involves a change of commitments and responsibilities. Ruth's conversion meant a whole new life in a new location. She even abandoned her native culture in order to join a people and serve their God, whose faith had radiated from Naomi even in tragedy.

Chapter 7

1 SAMUEL 17
David vs. Goliath

RSV   **Paraphrase**

17:1–11 The Philistines, Israel's archenemy, meet the Israelites for battle. They send out a huge, well-armed warrior, Goliath, to challenge any Israelite warrior to a one-on-one fight to the death. The winner's side will be declared sovereign over the other. Because Goliath is so imposing, this challenge embarrasses and discourages King Saul and his troops.

12–23 Young David, working as a shepherd for his father, is sent to the area where the Israelite troops are camped, with food and greetings for his brothers. While talking with his brothers he hears Goliath's challenge.

24–30 David is very much interested in the rewards, both personal and national, of defeating Goliath. He also wonders aloud why no one is willing to fight the Philistine. This angers his oldest brother, because it looks like David is goading the Israelites into combat while he himself has the luxury of being just a bystander, not appreciating the enormity of the challenge.

31–40 David convinces the initially skeptical King Saul that
he should be allowed to challenge Goliath. His main
argument is that God will aid him in this endeavor just
as he has in past dangers. After finding Saul's armor
unwieldy, David decides to face Goliath unarmed except for his sling.

41–47 Goliath mocks David, but David predicts victory because of his confidence in God.

48–54 David knocks out Goliath, kills him, and cuts off his
head. The encouraged Israelites rout the Philistines.

55–58 Saul takes great pains to learn about David's family
background as a prelude to arranging a marriage alliance between his own and David's family.

Introduction

The young shepherd's faith that God would give him victory over
so daunting an opponent and his victory in the name of God with
what seems to us a childish weapon have long captivated readers of
this chapter. David does, after all, what even the greatest Israelite
soldiers in Saul's army—and Saul himself—were afraid to do.

Some parts of the story have often been misunderstood, however,
and some clarification of these and the background in general can
help us to appreciate the account more fully.

It is also helpful to see how David shows the sort of faith that
allowed God to use him so effectively later as Israel's greatest king.
And here the cowardice of Saul, which progressively darkens into
disastrous leadership, is displayed at a relatively early juncture in
his career.

Vocabulary

17:1	*Socoh, Azekah, Ephes-dammim*	Towns in Judah. See below, Historical Setting.
4	*champion*	A warrior designated to fight instead of an entire army.
	cubits, span	See below, Biblical Context.

5	*coat of mail*	Special woven metal body armor.
	five thousand shekels	About 125 pounds.
6	*greaves*	Shin guards.
7	*six hundred shekels*	About 15 pounds.
	shield-bearer	A young soldier who carried the warrior's shield so the warrior had his hands free for using weapons.
8	*ranks*	Lined-up soldiers.
12	*Ephrathite*	Member of a certain Judean clan.
13	*followed Saul*	Joined Saul's army.
16	*forty*	This word is often used imprecisely to mean "a great many" rather than exactly forty.
17	*ephah*	Three fifths of a bushel.
	parched grain	Toasted grain, a popular food (cf. Ruth 2:14).
18	*thousand*	Company, platoon. Not actually one thousand soldiers.
	token	Something captured from the enemy indicating success in battle.
20	*host*	Army.
25	*free*	Free from taxes or other indebtedness.
29	*Was it not but a word?*	I didn't do anything but talk.
35	*beard*	Better: hair.
42	*disdained*	Despised.
52	*Gath, Ekron, Shaaraim*	Philistine cities.

Biblical Context

1 Samuel 17 is a flashback; that is, it recounts something that took place before the events which chapter 16 describes, not after them. Flashbacks are, of course, very commonly employed in modern books and movies as an effective way of providing background to a current situation. Telling everything in strict chronological order is not always the best way to get a story across, and therefore the inspired Bible writers sometimes shifted the order of presentation so as to place first things first. In the story of David, it is more important for Israel's history that he was anointed king by the prophet Samuel (chapter 16) than that he was the one who killed Goliath. So the anointing is told about first, and then the story flashes back to the Goliath incident. Other examples of flashbacks in the Bible include Jonah 4:5–11; Genesis 2:4–25; Esther 9:11–15; Acts 1:2–8 (compared to Luke 24:51–52).

David's use of a sling to knock out Goliath was not all that unusual a military tactic. Slinging was one of the arts of war in ancient times, and slinger-soldiers were formidable fighters. Judges 20:16 mentions the famed accuracy of the slingers of Benjamin; 2 Kings 3:25 describes how the conquest of a Moabite city was led by slingers. Slinging was thus young David's chosen fighting skill, the sort of skill against which a person of huge stature like Goliath had no special advantage.

Note that Goliath is never called a giant in this story or anywhere else in the Bible. Moreover, readings from the reliable ancient Dead Sea Scrolls and the Greek Old Testament (Septuagint) in 1 Samuel 17:4 say that Goliath was "four cubits and a span," not six cubits and a span. A cubit was the length from a man's elbow to the tip of his middle finger (about 18 inches). A span was the distance from thumb to little finger on an outstretched hand (about 9 inches). Thus there is good reason to believe that Goliath was about six feet nine inches tall—enormous in those days when adult males averaged five feet four, but not two or three times bigger than David, as artists' conceptions of this story sometimes show.

David was presumably in his mid to late teens at this time, not a child but not yet twenty years old. Twenty was the usual minimum fighting age (Numbers 1:3, 20, etc.). Like most Israelite men he would have been developing his fighting skills since childhood, but he would not yet have been expected to go into combat and thus was still shepherding while his oldest brothers were at war (1 Samuel 17:13–15).

The Philistines had presented the most constant military threat to the Israelites since the early days of the Judges. The stories of 1 Samuel are full of references to them (see especially chapters 4–7; 13–14). The Philistines occupied the coastal plain along the Mediterranean Sea, to the west, and kept trying to push inland to get more territory away from the Israelites. Israel's hold on the Promised Land was shaky, and Israel's tendency not to be faithful to God was a terrible mistake because it kept the Israelites from having God's support (Judges 2:11–15; 1 Samuel 12:25). They were already technologically inferior to the Philistines (1 Samuel 13:19–22) and were being driven back increasingly to the central Palestine hill country, as the Philistines took more and more of the fertile valleys away from them.

Historical Setting

Our story takes place about 1020 B.C., at a site (1 Samuel 17:1) roughly halfway between the Philistine city of Gath and the Judean city of Bethlehem—about ten miles from each. Ten miles was not a long walk for David, even up and down the winding paths from Bethlehem. Many other visitors and family members had surely made the same sort of trip that day to bring food to the troops and to see how they were faring. But David's attitude is different. He keeps mentioning the Lord and talking about what an insult was Goliath's constant, ongoing (v. 16) challenge to "the armies of the living God" (vs. 26, 36). Here David shows himself to be a person with deep, exclusive faith in Yahweh, Israel's only true God.

But weren't all the Israelites similarly faithful to Yahweh? By no means. Saul, for example, worshiped not only Yahweh but the Canaanite idol Baal, as the naming of one of his sons indicates (Esh-Baal, 1 Chronicles 8:33). The prophet Samuel had found it necessary in this era to call the Israelites away from worshiping Baal (1 Samuel 7:3–4), something they obviously had a long history of doing (1 Samuel 8:8; 12:10). David, however, was never involved in such compromise and thus is called a man after God's own heart (1 Samuel 13:14; Acts 13:22). His unshakable confidence in the true God was, unfortunately, the exception rather than the rule in his day.

Form and Structure

The chapter has a problem–solution sort of format, since that was the nature of the actual events. The challenge to Israel looks impossible to overcome at first (1 Samuel 17:1–11). David's arrival begins to get things off dead center (vs. 12–30). His decision to volunteer to fight Goliath and his victory (vs. 31–54) produce great interest in David on Saul's part (vs. 55–58), as a prelude to the reward David will get. What starts out as a humiliation ends up as a triumph—and the key ingredient is David's faith (vs. 26, 36, 37, 45–47).

Note that David and Goliath were running at each other when Goliath was felled by David's stone, not standing facing each other as pictures sometimes suggest (v. 48). Note also that Saul seems to be assuaging his own guilt by lending David his armor and sword (vs. 38–39). Saul, afraid himself to fight the Philistines' champion, at least can let David have the best armor and sword around—his own. David's intention all along was undoubtedly to use his sling against Goliath. The armor was intended for protection against Goliath's weapons at close range, and the sword for killing him if a stone would strike home and knock him out. What David really needed, though, was maneuverability for maximum accuracy. Goliath never got close enough to use his weapons against David; that was the idea.

It is important to realize that the Israelites did not exactly accept Goliath's terms. He proposed champion combat, acceptance of which would have allowed all the rest of the troops not to have to fight (v. 9), the losers simply agreeing to subservience. Instead, David fought him without any such conditions, and the Israelites attacked after David's victory in the same spirit (vs. 52–53). The order of God had been for full conquest of the Promised Land, not just for the suppression of its peoples (Deuteronomy 20:16–18).

Finally, Saul's questions about David's family (vs. 55–58) need to be seen in their proper significance. Undoubtedly, Saul's inquiries were much more detailed and are only summarized here for the sake of brevity in the narrative. He was making plans for allowing David to marry his daughter and for freeing David's family from taxes and so forth (v. 25; cf. 18:17–20). But he also had in mind the political advantages that a marriage alliance between his family, northerners, and David's family, southerners, would bring. Judah (the south) and

Israel (the north) tended to be somewhat suspicious of each other and often acted independently (e.g., 2 Samuel 2:8–11). Saul saw a chance to unite the two regions via blood ties, and David's marriage into royalty is an important aspect of David's career in its own right. Thus, as a result of his bravery against Goliath, David is "on his way to royalty" by the end of the story.

Application

1. Trust in God is of greater advantage than any weapon or strategy.
2. True faith gives one a different perspective on what can be accomplished in difficult situations.
3. The real hero of this story is God, as David himself acknowledges (1 Samuel 17:46–47).

Chapter 8

1 KINGS 3:16–28
Solomon's Wise Ruling

RSV   **Paraphrase**

3:16–22   Two prostitutes are fighting over a child, both claiming to be its mother. King Solomon is approached to make a ruling.

23   Solomon summarizes the essence of the case.

24–25   Solomon announces what sounds like his actual ruling.

26   One of the prostitutes appeals Solomon's "ruling" because the child is in fact hers.

27–28   Having gained the information he needed, the king makes his actual ruling, demonstrating his God-given wisdom.

Introduction

Quite a story! Among its ingredients are callousness, dishonesty, fraud, deception, remarkable perceptiveness, great anguish, true love, and true wisdom. Though the story is briefly told, it has such drama, such a positive, satisfying ending, and such a lesson for us about how God can help someone to make wise decisions that it has become one of the Old Testament's best-loved stories.

Vocabulary

3:16 *two harlots*

The Hebrew is better translated "two women who were prostitutes." The fact that they were prostitutes helps the reader understand how they might have been living together, without husbands, and how one of them might have been inept or careless enough to smother her own child as she slept. (In ancient times as in modern, good parenting was best learned in stable, loving homes. Prostitutes, unfortunately, do not usually come from such homes.)

But these prostitutes are still first of all *women*. And the story is concerned more with their instincts and needs as mothers than with their profession.

stood before him

This is technical language for appearing formally in the presence of the king for a court judgment.

20 *midnight*

The Hebrew term is better translated "in the middle of the night." No exact time is specified.

your maidservant

A term of humility, like "your humble servant."

in her bosom

Close to her, or at her side.

22 *Thus*

Not "Therefore" but "This is the way that . . ."

28	*all Israel*	An idomatic expression for: people from all over Israel. There is no implication that every Israelite actually heard this story.
	wisdom	The Hebrew term refers to the right application of knowledge.

Biblical Context

Wisdom was King Solomon's most famous attribute. This passage recounts a well-known illustration of that wisdom. Earlier in 1 Kings 3 (vs. 3–15) we are informed of the king's revelatory dream in which he asks God for wisdom more than any other divine gift. He wanted that wisdom not for selfish purposes but so that he might govern properly (v. 9). God did indeed grant Solomon's request (v. 12), and his decision about the disputed child confirmed his gift to the citizenry of this nation.

Solomon's reign is described in 1 Kings 1–11 and 2 Chronicles 1–9. It was a reign of forty years, characterized by great splendor and prestige, a time when Israel's influence internationally and its prosperity domestically were at high points. But Solomon's story is not always a positive one. Later in his life he grew to reject much of the very wisdom he had displayed in his governing judgments and in his collections of literary wisdom (Proverbs). 1 Kings 11:1–11 tells of his involvement in idolatry and polytheism, late in life, and the tragic results for his dynasty's lineage and for Israel as a nation. For Solomon, wisdom was a gift but not a guarantee. He was free to ignore his gift and eventually did so, leading his people away from orthodox religion (cf. Nehemiah 13:26).

Historical Setting

Solomon was king from 971 to 931 B.C., a time of relative peace because of the weakness of the area's major powers (Assyria, Babylonia, Egypt, Syria) and because of his father David's successful completion of the conquest of Canaan (2 Samuel 8), left incomplete during the days of the Judges (Judges 1:19–36).

Since Solomon had little need to lead Israelite armies in war (cf. 2 Samuel 11:1) he could devote relatively more attention to domestic responsibilities, including judging legal disputes.

In ancient Israel, kings were regularly involved in jurisprudence. People who had a legal disagreement were free to agree on any arbitrator they wished, and many agreed on the king, since a king's verdict had a finality that others' might not have. A king unavailable or untrustworthy to arbitrate disputes was in danger of losing his hold on the nation, and this is exactly what had happened to King David earlier (2 Samuel 15:2–6).

Today, even in such an influential Middle Eastern nation as Saudi Arabia, the king holds court several hours per week to hear legal cases directly from his citizens, who from the lowliest to the highest have access to him. Solomon was involved in the same duty when the two women were brought before him in Jerusalem to settle their dispute over child custody. Even common prostitutes had a right to seek a ruling from the king, and it was the king's responsibility to give it to them.

Here then was an opportunity for even obscure citizens to observe the king in action. When his God-given wisdom allowed Solomon to make such a clever judgment as is recorded in 1 Kings 3:16–28, this would obviously have enhanced his standing among his people and their confidence in him as a fitting monarch (v. 28).

Form and Structure

The passage is a historical narrative; that is, a story about an event that actually happened. Good storytelling requires keeping the central issues in focus and not letting the details obscure the impact. Our story, like biblical stories in general, is well-written: succinct, clear, simple, adequately but not overly detailed, and interesting.

The passage may be outlined easily:

1 Kings 3:16–22	Presentation of the case before Solomon
23–25	His clever *supposed* ruling
26–27	His *actual* ruling, based on the reaction to his supposed ruling
28	His expanded reputation for wisdom.

As the outline shows, it is the two rulings that the passage centers on. Verses 16–22 are what storytellers sometimes call the premise. They set the scene for us, so that we can see what a difficult decision Solomon had to make. When we come to the first ruling we are no more aware than the two women or the court attendants were that

Solomon has something up his sleeve, that he is announcing this ruling not because he seriously plans to have the child cut in half but because he wants to elicit a reaction.

Note the risk involved: The king could hardly be sure that both women would not accept his judgment. But it is helpful to realize that Solomon knew that there is a certain degree of predictability to human nature, and his God-given wisdom allowed him to exploit that relative predictability in a good way. Thus his *supposed* ruling yields immediately to his *actual* ruling, once he sees the reaction he was searching for: One woman shows true parental love and one sees the child simply as a possession.

A major concern of wisdom is the predictability of human nature. The book of Proverbs, for example, deals extensively with evaluating good habits and bad habits precisely because humans are in large measure creatures of habit; that is, to some extent predictable. The final part of the story (v. 28) reports that Solomon's ability to give justice was a gift of wisdom. In effect, he was held in "awe" because of his appreciation of human nature—an important asset in providing justice and equity to human beings.

Application

1. Wisdom is not only a matter of the development of normal human skills. True wisdom begins with obedience to God (cf. Proverbs 1:7).
2. People appreciate the unselfish use of wisdom to bring about fairness and justice.
3. Solomon's wisdom was extraordinary, given him specially by God, appropriately for his position. But the passage is written to encourage wisdom in us, too. God still gives wisdom to his people, appropriate to their tasks, if they earnestly seek it (James 1:5).

Chapter 9

1 KINGS 18:17–39
Elijah vs. the Prophets of Baal

RSV	Paraphrase
18:17–19	King Ahab accuses the prophet Elijah of being a troublemaker. Elijah responds by challenging the king to arrange a contest between the king's pagan prophets and himself, a lone true prophet.
20–24	After prophets and people gather at Mt. Carmel, Elijah issues the terms of the showdown: Whoever sends fire from heaven to consume a sacrifice will be proved the true God.
25–29	The prophets of Baal have the first chance, but after a day's sincere effort they can get no response from their god.
30–35	It is Elijah's turn. He puts his sacrificially prepared bull on a rebuilt ancient altar of the Lord and makes his task harder by dousing the sacrifice thoroughly with water.

36–38 At the end of the day, Elijah prays a simple prayer for the people, that they may be shown that they should turn back to the Lord from their idolatry. God sends fire, which consumes the offering, water, and even the stones of the altar.

39 The bystanders are convinced: The Lord is the true God.

Introduction

We live by faith and do not often have decisive proofs, even for the things we hold most dear. Nevertheless, when the occasion warrants it, God has been pleased to demonstrate his power from time to time in a dramatic and decisive way. We call these occasions miracles, and while they are infrequent they are an important part of the evidence that supports our faith.

As 1 Kings 18 opens, true religion is in danger of eradication at the hands of the wicked King Ahab and his foreign-born queen, Jezebel. Virtually no one other than Elijah was openly standing up for what was true. Something dramatic was needed, and God provided it in the famous contest at Mt. Carmel.

Vocabulary

18:17	*Ahab*	King of (northern) Israel from 874 to 853 B.C., remembered as its most corrupt, most pagan ruler (1 Kings 16:30).
	Elijah	The only aboveground true prophet of the Lord left at this time.
18	*your father's house*	Your father's family or dynasty.
	Baals	Various manifestations of the god of the elements, Baal. Baal was thought to be a divine specialist in rain, lightning, etc.
19	*all Israel*	People from all over Israel.

	Mount Carmel	A lush, high mountainous area on the northern Mediterranean coast of Israel.
	Asherah	Baal's divine girlfriend or mistress in the pagan mythology of the day.
	eat at Jezebel's table	Are on the queen's payroll. (Ahab's Phoenician wife, Jezebel, was an active supporter of Baal-Asherah religion and a fervent opponent of any worship of the Lord.)
20	*the prophets*	In fact, it was the Baal prophets who were chosen for the task (v. 22) in light of the fact that Baal's specialty in things like lightning seemed perfect for the occasion.
21	*limping with*	Crippled, handicapped by.
23	*the wood*	The wood ready to burn for cooking the sacrifice.
24	*answers by fire*	Sends fire down to ignite the wood.
	"It is well spoken."	"We like the idea."
25	*prepare it*	Bulls were butchered and cut up into parts for cooking. (A burnt offering was a cooked meal devoted to a god.)
	call on the name of	Pray specifically to. In a polytheistic society it was necessary to specify which god you were praying to or talking about.
26	*limped*	Hopped, jumped (part of their pagan ritual).
27	*musing*	Better: going to the bathroom.
	gone aside	Gone to do a bowel movement. (Elijah is certainly giving Baal a hard time.)

29	*offering of the oblation*	An evening offering.
30	*thrown down*	Destroyed by Jezebel's henchmen.
31	*Israel . . . your name*	Genesis 32:28.
32	*two measures*	About three and a half gallons.
37	*Answer me*	Respond to my prayer.
	turned their hearts back	Helped them to believe in you again.
39	*fell on their faces*	In the posture of worship, flat on the ground.
	he is God	That is, as opposed to Baal.

Biblical Context

The stories about Elijah and his successor Elisha occupy a prominent position in 1 and 2 Kings (1 Kings 17 to 2 Kings 13). These two fiercely devout spokesmen for the Lord had dealings frequently with Israel's kings, often at great risk to themselves. Together they helped stem the tide of paganism in Israel, though the strength of that tide never receded entirely, and pagan beliefs and practices eventually were the cause of Israel's downfall (2 Kings 17).

Elijah was an intriguing character. He is known both for his miracle-working and for his tender compassion toward the needy (1 Kings 17:8–24). He was subject to the same peaks of victory and valleys of discouragement (1 Kings 19:1–14) that we are, and yet he played a key role in God's plan—especially in terms of his famous prayers for drought and rain (James 5:17–18).

Historical Setting

Israel and Judah had split off from each other after the death of Solomon in 931 B.C. (1 Kings 12). In Israel, after a bloody struggle, Omri established himself as king in 885 B.C. and moved the capital to Samaria. His son Ahab led the nation officially away from the worship of the Lord (it had been drifting unofficially away from the Lord for some time) and allowed his wife, Jezebel, to attempt to exterminate the Lord's prophets so that the new state religion of Baal and Asherah could prevail (1 Kings 18:4, 13).

Internationalism was the emphasis of the day. Ahab wanted to break Israel out of the narrow, unusual, restrictive religion of the Lord and make it like the other nations, with their polytheism and their idolatry. He might have succeeded, but for the brave loyalty to God displayed by Elijah and for the contest God won, described here in 1 Kings 18.

Form and Structure

The drought and rain story surrounds our passage. The form of our passage is historical narrative, and we often find a narrative within a narrative, as is the case here. Our narrative, the story of the contest on Mt. Carmel, is set within the larger narrative of the drought and rain. God had told Elijah to pray for a lack of rain as a punishment to the Israelites for turning to the worship of Baal (1 Kings 17:1). This was especially appropriate because Baal, as the supposed god of the elements, was believed to be in charge of the rain. Therefore, when it was widely known that Elijah had prayed to *the Lord* to withhold rain, and drought indeed resulted, Baal worshipers like Ahab were greatly embarrassed.

The drought lasted three years and brought great hardship. That is why Ahab calls Elijah the "troubler of Israel" in 1 Kings 18:17. But God's purpose was to teach Israel a lesson, not to harm it just for the sake of bringing harm. So right after Elijah's victory on Mt. Carmel, God announces through him to none other than that rascal, Ahab, that "there is a sound of the rushing of rain" (v. 41). In fact, Elijah tells Ahab that there will eventually be so much rain that unless he gets to the city of Jezreel fast, his chariot will not make it through the mud (v. 44). The drought was ending.

The drought–rain story and our contest story within it are evidences of God's love. He wants the best for his people, even when they have turned against him. His concern is to bless them by turning them back to himself (v. 37), which is what they desperately need, whether they know it or not. As soon as he has made this point, he sends his rain.

Application

1. The Lord is the only God. Sincere faith in other gods is sincere faith in nothing (1 Kings 18:29).
2. God wants people to turn to him not for the sake of his pride, but so that he might bless them.

Chapter 10

2 KINGS 22
Josiah and the Book of the Law

RSV	Paraphrase
22:1–2	Josiah became king at the tender age of eight and yet was religiously entirely faithful to the Lord, as King David had been.
3–7	In the eighteenth year of his kingship he launched a project to renovate the temple. Knowing that the work was being properly done, he sent his secretary to instruct the high priest to pay the workmen accordingly.
8–10	At the temple the high priest told the secretary of a major find—an old "foundation deposit" copy of the Law from the days of Solomon when the temple was built. Shaphan read the book to King Josiah.
11–13	The king saw at once that God's word had not been kept and therefore that the nation was in rebellion against God, deserving God's wrath. He ordered that his officials should consult a prophet to learn God's decision about their nation.

14–20 They sought out the woman Huldah, a prophet there in the city of Jerusalem. Through her, God told them that the punishments predicted in his law would indeed come to pass in light of the nation's history of sin, but not until after the death of King Josiah.

Introduction

The passage 2 Kings 22 is about the impact of reading the Bible. King Josiah probably had about the same vague idea of what was in the Law of God that the average American would have. When he then heard an entire Pentateuch book read to him from beginning to end, the impression was overwhelming. He realized for the first time how far he and his nation were from the standards God had set for them, and how dangerous it was to keep on in the direction they had been going.

The discovery of a book of the Law and Josiah's response sparked an enormous revival of orthodoxy in Judah and a long-needed systematic cleanup of religious and ethical practices among the people (2 Kings 23).

Vocabulary

22:1	*his mother's name*	This is important because the queen mother was a more significant figure than any of the king's wives in Israel.
2	*right in the eyes of*	Proper from the viewpoint of.
	walked in all the way	Acted in the same manner as.
	his father	His ancestor.
	did not turn aside . . . right . . . left	Was consistently honest and upright.
3	*secretary*	Royal official, cabinet member; not just a taker of dictation or a typist.
4	*reckon*	Figure up.

	keepers of the threshold	Temple ushers or guards.
7	*accounting*	Proof of how the money was spent. (This was a compliment to Josiah; he could trust people to be loyal and honest because of his own favor among the people.)
8	*the book of the law*	Either the entire Pentateuch or, more likely, the book of Deuteronomy (judging from the vocabulary used in referring to it later in 2 Kings).
11	*rent*	Tore (symbolic of being grieved and appealing to God).
12	*king's servant*	A royal official, not a minor worker.
13	*inquire of the LORD*	This usually means: consult a prophet.
	the wrath . . . kindled	The anger that is building.
	concerning us	Concerning our nation, our people.
14	*keeper of the wardrobe*	Shallum, Huldah's husband, was in charge of the temple priests' garments.
	Second Quarter	A section of the old city of Jerusalem.
16	*evil*	Better: trouble, or harm.
	this place	Judah.
17	*burned incense*	Better: burned offerings.
	all the work of their hands	Everything they do.
19	*a curse*	A thing cursed by God.
	I also have heard you	I also have decided to respond positively to you.

20	*gather you to your fathers*	Cause you to join your ancestors in the next world.
	gathered to your grave in peace	Die and be burned after a satisfying life.

Biblical Context

Josiah was not the only Israelite leader to be called back to orthodoxy by hearing God's word. The Law of Moses was the document that structured proper Israelite (Judean) behavior at all times—when it was obeyed, that is.

In our passage, the roles of the priest Hilkiah and the prophet Huldah are very important ones. For a knowledge of the law to be kept alive, someone has to make it a point to know that law and to disseminate its teachings. Those priests and prophets who were still faithful to the Lord fulfilled this role in ancient Israel.

It should not surprise us that the content of something as foundational as the law of God should not be widely known and could therefore come as a revelation to the king. Consider how important, for example, the Constitution of the United States is and yet how few people can recite—or even recognize—most of its contents. There are, however, specialists who do know the Constitution well and who keep it alive, as it were: judges and constitutional lawyers.

Huldah was a specialist of a somewhat different sort, however, because her expertise went beyond a mere acquaintance with the law. She was a person called by God to speak his word to her contemporaries in terms of how and when God's law would be enforced. Now that Josiah and his associates knew clearly the penalties for the sort of neglect of righteousness that had been ongoing for centuries before their time (cf. 1 Kings 11–21), they needed to know if there was any hope at all for them. The sorts of disasters predicted in Deuteronomy 28–32 for an ungodly nation—which they surely were at the time and had long been—were awesome: defeat in war, great suffering, and deportation, just to name a few.

Was there then any hope? Did they have a chance? If they repented and turned to God, would he be interested, or was he fed up? The great need for an answer to these questions is what drove them to Huldah, a known and trusted spokesperson for God.

Historical Setting

It was 622 B.C. when the workmen repairing the temple found the book of the Law. Such a document was not just lying around in a storeroom somewhere but was undoubtedly recovered from one of the temple's foundation deposits.

In ancient times buildings did not have signs, plaques, room directories, or that sort of thing. Instead, the significance and purpose of a building was indicated by materials placed right into the building's structure. Sometimes the bricks or woodwork were inscribed; in the case of temples, appropriate materials were sealed into a hollow chamber in the foundation. Since the book of Deuteronomy specifies the need for a temple (Deuteronomy 12), Solomon would surely have included a scroll of this book among the materials placed in the foundation deposit(s) of the temple he built in 971 B.C. (1 Kings 6).

Have you ever seen handwriting from several centuries ago (such as in a copy of the Declaration of Independence) and noticed how different it is from our own? That is the sort of experience the high priest Hilkiah had when the workmen brought the scroll they had just found in the foundation under repair. It was at least three and a half centuries old by that time, and Hilkiah saw in it the handwriting style and spelling of an ancient document.

The king of course was curious to hear how this ancient document sounded—even though he could have heard it from plenty of copies available from his own day—and for the first time in his life he listened to a whole book of the Law with real interest and comprehension. The result was a grievous conviction that the punishments prescribed for the nation that disobeyed God's law (Deuteronomy 28–32) were already long overdue against Judah.

Form and Structure

You will notice in the passage a relatively small amount of description and a relatively large amount of dialogue. This proportion of description to dialogue is quite different from some kinds of modern narrative writing but is remarkably typical for Old Testament narrative. The Bible does not usually give you descriptions of sunsets, the physical appearance of people or their facial expressions, and so forth. In fact it almost never sets the scene in any elaborate way. Instead it provides the bare necessary facts and concentrates on summarizing the essential developments, including conversation.

In 2 Kings 22 dialogue is prominent. Verses 4–7, the king's statement, set up the situation under which the royal secretary would come in contact with the newly found scroll. The announcement of the find itself comes via the statement of the high priest in verse 8 and is reported to the king by Shaphan's words quoted in verses 9 and 10. Thereafter, in verse 13 the king's words provide for consulting the Lord via Huldah. Now, as we might imagine, the most important quotation in any dialogue would be the quotation of God himself. And that is exactly what we find here. The climax of the chapter is the speech of God through Huldah in verses 15–20. There we find the answer to the concern raised by the king in verse 13 ("Great is the wrath of the LORD"): God's wrath is great, but it will be delayed until after Josiah dies.

Application

1. God's word must be taken seriously.
2. There is nothing like actually reading God's word for impact upon our lives.
3. Good leaders recognize that God's favor is essential if they are to lead well.

Chapter 11

EZRA 6
Rebuilding the Temple

RSV	Paraphrase
6:1–5	At the command of Darius, king of Persia (522–486 B.C.), various document storage centers were searched until a forgotten decree from a previous Persian king, Cyrus (539–530 B.C.), was found. This decree authorized the rebuilding of the Jerusalem temple, which had been stripped of its valuables and destroyed (in 586 B.C.) by the Babylonians.
6–12	On the basis of the decree, King Darius demanded that various officials from regions bordering Judah not only should stop harassing the Jews in their rebuilding effort but should provide the funds for it from the district royal tax income. Failure to obey would have the most severe consequences.
13–15	The various non-Jewish officials did obey, and work on the temple went ahead full speed, just as the prophets Haggai and Zechariah had prophesied that it must. The temple was completed in 516 B.C.

16–18   The people had a grand dedication ceremony for the temple, with many sacrifices and the reinstitution of the full temple priesthood.

19–22   The next month they celebrated the feast of Passover, properly undertaken by all who were worthy. That Passover week was a joyous one, because of all God had done for them, including influencing the king to support the rebuilding.

Introduction

The Jerusalem temple was the center of Israel's worship (cf. Deuteronomy 12). But as Ezra 6 opens, the temple lies in ruins, only its foundation having been completed. The Jews are afraid to do any more work on it because powerful neighbor states have threatened them, knowing that a rebuilt temple might inspire the Jews to national pride and then to a reassertion of their old domination of the area. But God knows how to get his house of worship built. Even kings, after all, are under his control. And indeed the great king himself, Darius, ends up not only ordering the rebuilding of the temple but paying for it.

This delightful story of God's encouragement to a struggling community of returned exiles has always warmed the hearts of God's people.

Vocabulary

6:2	*Media*	A nation to the east of Mesopotamia. It merged with Persia in the Persian Empire.
3	*cubits*	A cubit is about 18 inches, so the rough dimensions of the temple were to be 90 feet by 90 feet.
4	*great stones*	Large stone building blocks.
	royal treasury	The king's tax collection in the district.

5	*Nebuchadnezzar*	The Babylonian king whose armies conquered Jerusalem and destroyed its temple in 586 B.C.
6	*Beyond the River*	The Persian-Aramaic name of Palestine.
7	*elders*	Leaders.
8	*tribute*	Royal tax.
9	*wheat, salt, wine, oil*	Also sacrifice ingredients. Sacrifices produced balanced meals, including wine to drink, which were shared by the priests and worshipers.
11	*beam . . . impaled*	This was a serious warning. Darius had "crucified" thousands of opponents just this way in the city of Babylon alone.
12	*caused his name to dwell there*	See 1 Kings 8:16–20, 27–29.
14	*Artaxerxes*	A later Persian king (464–424 B.C.), during whose reign Nehemiah rebuilt Jerusalem's walls.
15	*Adar*	The last month in the year, mid-February to mid-March.
	sixth year	516 B.C.
16	*Levites*	The clergy tribe to which all priests belonged.
18	*courses*	Work shifts.
19	*first month*	Mid-March to mid-April, the beginning of spring.
21	*pollutions of the peoples of the land*	Sins and practices of the nearby population not allowed by the Law of Moses.
22	*feast of unleavened bread*	The Passover feast (cf. Leviticus 23:5–8).

| *king of Assyria* | A general term for the king of Persia, since the old Assyrian Empire was in the hands of the Persians. |

Biblical Context

The actual words spoken by Haggai and Zechariah to encourage the Jews to get back to work on the temple are found in the books of Haggai (both chapters) and Zechariah (chapters 1–8 especially). They are strong words, full of warnings about the dangers of neglect, but there are promises of grandeur to come if the little band of returned exiles will only go ahead with the work on the temple (e.g., Haggai 1:2–10; 2:21–23).

Naturally, group action of the sort called for has to have leadership. The Jewish governor of Judah at the time, Zerubbabel, and the high priest, Jeshua, were thus key figures in the rebuilding efforts (Ezra 5:2) and are the direct subjects of many of the promises and encouragements in the books of Haggai and Zechariah.

But Ezra 6 tells us who the real hero was: God himself, who had decided that this temple was going to wait no longer to be rebuilt.

Once the temple was finished, the proper worship so necessary to bind the community of faith together could recommence (6:16–22). It had been a long time since the Passover had been celebrated— seventy years, in fact, from the destruction of the first temple to the completion of the second (cf. Jeremiah 29:10). But a new beginning had indeed been made. The very temple at which Jesus himself would teach (Luke 20:1) and which he would cleanse (Matthew 21:12) hundreds of years later was complete.

Historical Setting

It was 520 B.C. Judah, like the rest of the Near East, was under the domination of the Persians. A new king, Darius, had been in power just over a year. Before Darius the Persian Empire had been in an uproar as a result of various civil and military disturbances and the inability of Darius's weak predecessors to do much about it.

Judah's neighbors had taken advantage of the confusion back in Persia to put a stop to the Jews' efforts in Jerusalem to get the temple rebuilt. There had been a good start (Ezra 3) in 537 B.C., but for seventeen years the opposition had succeeded in preventing any further progress (Ezra 4).

Then in 520 B.C. God moved the two prophets Haggai and
Zechariah, the same two whose books are among the Minor Prophets, to urge the Jews to trust in God's protection, ignore their
neighbor's threats, and get back to the rebuilding of the temple (Ezra
5:1–2).

Immediately a local Persian Empire district governor, Tattenai,
along with other local officials including the influential
Shetharbozenai, complained by letter to Darius (Ezra 5:3–17). The
Jews were claiming that the first king of the Persian Empire, Cyrus,
had given them permission to build (Ezra 1). The letter asked Darius
to try to confirm this, assuming of course that he couldn't. But he
did (6:1–4), and the opposition was squelched.

On their own the Jews could have done very little. They had been
back in Palestine from exile in Mesopotamia only eighteen years and
were economically poor and few in number. As a military threat
they were a joke. Only by God's grace could the events of chapter
6 ever have taken place.

Form and Structure

Ezra 6 contains quotations from two important documents, the
original edict of King Cyrus (vs. 3–5) and the letter to Tattenai and
Shetharbozenai from King Darius (vs. 6–12).

These two quotations, along with most of the rest of the chapter,
are written in Aramaic, which was the standard diplomatic and
international trade language of that day, much as English is in our
day. It is not known exactly why some parts of the book of Ezra are
written in Aramaic while the rest is in Hebrew. Perhaps the author,
who may well have been Ezra himself, started with original records
of various sorts in Aramaic, then added to them in Hebrew. Ezra, in
fact, did not arrive in Judah from Mesopotamia until 458 B.C. (see
Ezra 7), so that the events described in chapter 6—around 520
B.C.—preceded him by more than half a century.

Note that the chapter begins in suspense—What will be the result
of the search? Can the original records be found after the long delay
and all the turmoil in previous Persian administrations?—but ends in
confidence. Free and secure, the Jews can once again follow the
Law of Moses.

Application

1. Even the greatest of the world's leaders are ultimately under God's control.
2. Confidence in God may require going ahead with something even in the face of strong opposition.
3. God is faithful to his word (Ezra 1:1–4; 6:22), in spite of changes in human affairs.

Chapter 12

JOB 1
The Testing of Job

RSV	Paraphrase
1:1–5	Job from Uz was righteous and rich and loved his family deeply.
6–12	Satan, in conversation with God, charges that Job is righteous only because he has prospered so much. God agrees to allow Satan to take away all that Job has, except his life and health, to test Job's faithfulness under adverse conditions.
13–19	Four disasters then befall Job: (1) his cattle are stolen and some of his servants are killed; (2) his sheep and some servants are burned up; (3) his camels are stolen and some servants are killed; (4) his children are killed.
20–22	Job laments his loss but remains righteous, faithful to God.

Introduction

Job's story is a moving one. He had everything and, through no fault of his own, lost it all—family, possessions, everything. Yet he still remained faithful to God. In this, without ever knowing, he proved God right and Satan wrong. Satan assumed, as many people might, that religious individuals are actually religious for selfish reasons; that is, because somehow it pays to be religious. This need not be the case, however, as Job demonstrates by continuing to be righteous after experiencing great loss.

Vocabulary

1:1	*Uz*	A land east of ancient Canaan, probably located near Edom, a neighboring territory to Israel. (See Genesis 36:28; Jeremiah 25:20; and Lamentations 4:21.) Note that Job was not a Hebrew.
	feared God	Was truly religious. The Bible almost never uses the adjective "religious" but, instead, emphasizes a serious devoted relationship to God by using the term "fear."
3	*Yoke of oxen*	Pairs of oxen, one thousand in all.
	servants	Also: slaves.
	greatest of all	A rather typical exaggeration (cf. Matthew 13:32). Our modern English equivalent: one of the most prominent, or the like.
4	*on his day*	The feast took a week, probably once a year. Each of the seven days, the feasting would be at a different son's house.
5	*sanctify them*	Ritually prepare so that they would be clean and pure, ready to offer an acceptable sacrifice. Involved in the

		sanctifying process were ceremonial washings, proper dress, and abstinence from things ritually unclean such as dead or diseased animals.
	my sons	Better: my children. The gender in the Hebrew is unspecified.
	in their hearts	Job knew no outward irreligious behavior on the part of his children but was still concerned that in attitude or thought they might have displeased God.
	continually	On a regular basis, year by year; not constantly.
6	*sons of God*	A common term for angels, whether heavenly or fallen (cf. Genesis 6:2; Daniel 3:25).
7	*up and down on it*	An idiom for: spending time attending to business on earth.
9	*for nought*	Emptily, for no reason.
11	*touch*	Better: plague or harm.
	to thy face	Directly or openly. The wording does not imply that God is visible.
12	*do not put forth your hand*	Don't lay a finger on him personally.
15	*Sabeans*	Marauders from Sheba, in southwest Arabia, the same nation whose queen visited Solomon (1 Kings 10:1–10).
16	*fire of God*	The term can refer to lightning, but fire in general signifies destructive judgment (cf. Deuteronomy 32:22; Amos 1:4, 7, 10, etc.), which would have suggested to others that Job's distresses must be punishments for some sin(s) he had committed.

17	*Chaldeans*	An Aramaean (Syrian) ethnic group.
19	*struck the four corners*	The wind was a destructive whirlwind, not just a prevailing wind.
	young people	Job's children.
20	*rent his robe*	Tore his robe in one or more places to indicate mourning. When people mourned before God in ancient times, they did not want to seem well dressed and comfortable, so they ruined their clothes and made themselves symbolically disfigured by putting dirt on themselves (Job 2:12) or shaving off their hair.
	fell upon the ground	People did not merely bow at the waist or kneel to show subservience in ancient times; they often stretched out prostrate on their faces (e.g., Ezra 10:1).
21	*return*	Not return to his mother's womb, of course, but return to the earth, to the dust (cf. Job 3:17).

Biblical Context

Job is a big book, and chapter 1 is only half of its beginning section, usually called the Prologue (chs. 1–2). The story of chapter 1 sets the scene for the entire story, however. The book as a whole teaches a very important lesson: This life is not fair. Good people can suffer without having done anything to deserve their suffering. Bad people can prosper without having done anything to deserve their prosperity.

Most of the book relates discussions (dialogues) between Job and several of his friends. The friends all reflect the view that this life *is* fair, that God would not allow such disasters to happen to Job unless he had sinned. So they constantly defend the fairness of life to Job, assuming that they are thereby defending God's fairness. Thus they keep trying to get Job to confess the sin they assume he is hiding. Job, in return, consistently asserts his righteousness and demonstrates that, while we cannot understand why, this life is just not necessarily fair.

God finally speaks to Job directly (Job 38–41), and then approves of Job's position as over against that of his friends (42:7–8). But Job never finds out that his miseries happened in order that God might be vindicated and that Job's own uprightness and deep religious faith might be proved true and unselfish. What God does tell Job in chapters 38–41 is in effect very simple but very powerful: "I know what I'm doing. Trust me." Job never learns the answers to all the questions he asks in chapters 3–31; what he learns is that God is in control of things and knows what he's doing.

The book of Job is wisdom literature, a special category of literature in ancient times. The most prominent characteristic of "wisdom" as a way of thinking was its awareness that all of life involves choices. Wisdom literature often concentrated on these choices: the wise (right) way of doing things as opposed to the foolish (ungodly) way.

Proverbs is perhaps best-known among the Old Testament books as a wisdom book, but Ecclesiastes, some psalms (e.g., Psalms 37; 49; 73; 112; 127; 128; 133) and parts of some prophetical books (e.g., Hosea 14:9) or historical books (e.g., 1 Samuel 24:13) also contain wisdom teachings. Job comes under the general category known as "speculative wisdom" because it is a dialogue-style poetic story in which there is a lot of theoretical discussion—"speculation"—about the choices of life and their rightness or wrongness. Job's view, that by choosing to do right one still cannot necessarily avoid suffering, proves to be correct. But we read a lot of carefully composed speculation on both sides of that issue before we learn this important answer.

Historical Setting

The evidence suggests that Job lived in the days of the so-called patriarchs (men such as Abraham, Isaac, and Jacob); that is, sometime around 2000–1500 B.C. The measurement of wealth by cattle and servants in the chapter reflects patriarchal practice (cf. Genesis 12:16; 32:5). The fact that Job offers his own sacrifices (Job 1:5) compares to patriarchal practice as well (e.g., Genesis 22). The Sabeans and Chaldeans (Job 1:15, 17) are not yet settled, as would be the case later, but are still marauding nomads. Job's long life (42:16–17) compares with that of the patriarchs (e.g., Genesis

35:28–29), and the coinage mentioned in 42:11 is a very old one (Genesis 33:19).

Thus the story is about a great person (see Ezekiel 14:20) from an age far in the past to most of its readers. His faithfulness to God "way back then" was a lesson to later generations who heard or read his story.

Form and Structure

In this passage we observe some interesting repetitions that show how stylized (composed according to a set format) the chapter is.

Note first that in verses 1 and 22—that is, the beginning and the end of the chapter—Job's righteousness before God is emphasized. He starts out righteous and ends up righteous, in spite of all that happens in between. Note also that twice he is called righteous by the use of four synonyms (blameless, upright, feared God, turned from evil): in verse 1 by the narrator and also in verse 8 by God. There is also a bit of a "7 and 3" pattern in verses 2 and 3, produced probably by approximating the numbers and perhaps, in the case of the animals, even the ratios. Moreover, the speeches of those who escape the four disasters described in verses 14–19 are remarkably similar ("I alone have escaped to tell you," etc.).

The main purpose for this stylized language is emphasis. The repetitions of set phrases drive home the points that Job was truly righteous and truly wealthy and that the misfortunes that befell him were truly disastrous. This is an effective technique in storytelling and helps the reader appreciate the significance of these factors in Job's life.

Overall, chapter 1 is a historical narrative in form. The book of Job employs prose historical narrative for chapters 1 and 2 and the end (vs. 7–17) of chapter 42. Otherwise the book is poetry, in which Job's lengthy conversations with his friends and even with God are conveyed in poetic form. Many great works of literature have been all or mostly poetic (Dante's *Inferno,* Shakespeare's plays, Milton's *Paradise Lost,* T. S. Eliot's *The Waste Land*), though in recent years poetic storytelling in Western culture has concentrated mostly on musical poetry. Musicals like *Oklahoma* or *My Fair Lady* or *Annie* tell their stories with poetry set to music—lyrics—because there is a special sort of audience appeal to such a literary form. In ancient times poetry was especially popular as a medium for storytelling, and Job reflects its popularity.

Application

1. Is this life unfair? Absolutely. Evil often prevails and good is often suppressed or goes unrewarded. The importance of a final judgment (Matthew 25:31–46; Revelation 20:11–15; etc.) is thus underscored. God will, in the life to come, make all things the way they should be.
2. Must we have a pleasant life in order to have the endurance to do God's will? Absolutely not. Our calling is to be faithful in spite of—as well as because of—what this life brings our way.
3. Can we know why we suffer? Usually not. But we can know, with Job, that God knows—and cares.

Chapter 13

PSALM 8
Less than the Angels

RSV	Paraphrase
[super-scrip-tion]	A psalm written by David, from the temple choirmaster's collection, to be sung to a tune called "The Gittith."
8:1–2	The Lord's authority is so great that his universal glory is sung even by the cries and cooing of babies. He protects the righteous against the wicked.
3–4	In comparison with the magnificence of the universe God created, why should he care about human beings?
5–8	But he does, and has made them only a little less than the angels: glorious, with control over the animal world.
9	The Lord's authority is so great!

Introduction

Here is a beloved Bible hymn that pays special attention to the significance of human beings in the order of things, while at the same time reminding us that God is greater still.

It is a reflective, thoughtful hymn, in which God is praised precisely because he has given humans such an elevated position in his creation. And there is also the element of sheer wonder at what an amazing thing it is to be so loved and favored by God.

So it is a hymn about us, but only insofar as it is a hymn about God.

Vocabulary

super-scrip-tion:	"The Gittith"	An unknown tune, possibly meaning something like "By the Winepress."
8:1	*chanted*	Better: given forth. The babies are not actually thought to sing.
2	*bulwark*	A strong, protective arrangement.
4	*man*	A human being, not a man as distinct from a woman.
	care for	Care about, pay attention to.
5	*God*	The Hebrew term can also mean angels or heavenly beings, and is taken this way by most ancient versions.
6	*under his feet*	In his control.
7	*beasts of the field*	Wild animals in general.
8	*paths of the sea*	Ocean channels, currents, etc.

Biblical Context

The most intriguing aspect of this hymn is the statement in verse 5, "Yet thou hast made him little less than God" (RSV) or ". . . the angels" (KJV). Here in a brief poetic turn of phrase an important biblical truth is summarized.

Human beings do indeed occupy a special position in the earthly creation. They alone are made in God's image, which means that they have a special responsibility and authorization to have dominion over the earth and its animal and plant life (see v. 6, and chapter 1, "The Creation Is Good").

But they are not—yet—at the level of angels and other supernatural beings. Angels were part of a creation prior to our own and have their own relationship to God with its own responsibilities. One day humans, in heaven, will have some authority over angels (1 Corinthians 6:3). For now, however, we are a "little less than" they.

By the way, the Hebrew word translated "little" can also mean "a little while," and both meanings may be present in verse 5: we are a little less than heavenly beings for a little while.

The point is, of course, that we are in a high position indeed! There is an order to creation, with God at the top, heavenly beings below him, us below them, animals below us, and so forth. But "below" need not mean of lower concern or value. All of God's creation is good (Genesis 1), and the fact that humans are *lower* than angels does not mean they are less loved or cared for (Psalm 8:4).

Historical Setting

Psalm 8 is, like many psalms, panhistorical, not limited by time or culture. It talks about basic relationships that have always existed since creation.

As a psalm of David (if the superscription is accurate—and this is only an assumption, since the superscriptions were added after the psalms were written and are therefore not even given verse numbers in the Bible), it might have been composed sometime around 1000 B.C. (David reigned from 1011 B.C. to 971 B.C.) It would therefore be one of the earliest psalms in the Bible, while at the same time being one of the most contemporary in every age, including our own, because of its enduring truths.

Form and Structure

The various types of psalms have their own formats. A hymn, which emphasizes the reasons God deserves praise, usually has an introduction (here the first part of v. 1), a main body, describing what God is and does, and a conclusion (here v. 9). In Psalm 8 the introduction and conclusion are identical, as is common (similarly in Psalms 103; 104; 106; 113; 118; etc.).

Here the main body is centered upon God's creation of human beings in such a way that they are the "crown" (Ps. 8:5) of that creation. After the introduction, praising God's name (= authority/identity), we read in sequence that everything in God's creation is rightly a glorifying force for him—even babies' cries (vs. 1–2); he restrains evil (v. 2); it is amazing that God should pay such attention to humans—but he does (vs. 3–4), having placed them in a superior position in the creation "order" (vs. 5–8); and finally that, just as the psalm said at the beginning, God's name is praiseworthy.

It is a simple format but a powerful one.

Application

1. When we think about the uniqueness and greatness of human beings in our world, it should remind us also of *God's* uniqueness and greatness.
2. Our important position in the creation order carries with it an important responsibility—dominion over the things God has created.
3. Our world is as stable as it is because God restrains its evil (Psalm 8:2).

Chapter 14

PSALM 23
God Cares

RSV	Paraphrase
23:1–3	The Lord takes care of me as a good shepherd would take care of one of his sheep.
4	As the shepherd keeps his sheep from danger, so you, Lord, keep me from danger.
5–6	You are my host who accepts me. I can be confident of the future.

Introduction

Here is the Old Testament's best-known passage. We love this psalm because it gives us deep reassurance. It reminds us by means of several comparisons that God really does watch over us and care for us.

The basic sense of the psalm is something anyone can comprehend and delight in. Nevertheless, there are features visible in the original, including the meanings of some words, that do not automatically come across in the English translation.

Vocabulary

23:1 *want*

Need anything I already have. "Want" is used here in the old sense of lack, rather than desire. *Note:* "The Lord is my shepherd" and "I shall not want" are related causally. This could also be translated "Because the Lord is my shepherd I shall not want." The technical term for this type of grammar is asyndeton, which refers to a logical connection between statements that are not visibly connected by a conjunction.

2 *makes me lie down*

A single verb in the Hebrew that means, in effect: lets me settle down. The Shepherd's job is to find the lush pasturage and bring the sheep to it. They settle in automatically.

still waters

Waters of rest or peacefulness. The Shepherd finds places for the sheep to drink where they will not be molested or endangered. There is nothing intended here about the depth of the water or how fast it flows.

3 *soul*

The Hebrew means "life." The point is not that the sheep has a spiritual experience (soul) but that he or she has been brought by the Shepherd to a place where his or her strength is revived and he or she can go on living.

paths of righteousness

Proper paths, the ones that keep the sheep from becoming lost or harmed.

his name's sake

For the sake of who he is. The Shepherd is Yahweh, whose "name" (authority, identity, honor) means that he can be trusted to be gracious.

4	*valley of the shadow of death*	Pitch-dark valley. Death per se is not mentioned, but a dark valley at nightfall would be a potentially deadly place for sheep, so the translation is not essentially misleading.
	comfort	Reassure.
5	*enemies*	Any persons or things that threaten, not particularly enemies in war.
	anointest	Anointing was the practice of wetting head and facial hair with oil (usually olive oil) to kill lice. Lice were epidemic in ancient times, and oil was the best delousing agent. Oil thus symbolized cleanness and freedom from infection. A loving host provided water for his guests to wash with upon arriving at the house. A very loving host might also provide oil, expensive though it was, so that the guest would be most graciously cared for and comfortable.
	overflows	Not with oil, but wine. The host is shown here to be *very* generous.
6	*surely*	The Hebrew term also means only, an even stronger promise.
	mercy	Loyalty. The emphasis is on God's faithfulness to us.
	days of my life	An idiomatic expression for "all my life" in Hebrew, this does not connote "one day at a time" or any such thing.
	I shall dwell	The Hebrew is a clever combination of verbs meaning return and dwell. It refers to frequent worship rather than actual residence at God's house.

for ever   The Hebrew is literally "for length of
                                      days"; that is, "my life long." The
                                      doctrine of eternal life, well
                                      established elsewhere in the Bible, is
                                      not mentioned specifically here. It is,
                                      of course, not specifically excluded
                                      either.

Biblical Context

The Psalter contains various types of musical poems: laments,
songs of thanksgiving, hymns, royal songs, wisdom psalms, etc.
Psalm 23 is part of a group called songs of trust. Nine other songs are
found in this category: Psalms 11; 16; 27:1–6; 62; 63; 91; 121; 125;
131.

The psalms are not grouped in the Bible by category, for the most
part, but somewhat randomly—the way hymns are grouped in many
of our modern hymnals. Therefore the context of a hymn—that is,
its position among other hymns—is usually insignificant. Psalm 23
does not build upon Psalm 22 or lead into Psalm 24. It is a
self-contained unit, with its closest parallels in the psalms listed
above, not those near to it in the Psalter.

Here is what songs of trust typically contain:

Reference to the nearness of God

Reference to God's power to protect or save

Reference to worship or praise at God's house

An overall sense that confidence in God is not misplaced

These elements may come in any order or proportion. One
element or another may remain implicit rather than actually being
stated by the psalmist. But usually when you see these kinds of
elements being expressed throughout a psalm (and not just in part of
a psalm), you will recognize a song of trust. Other types of psalms
do contain expressions of trust (almost all lament psalms do, for
example), but only songs of trust concentrate throughout on confidence in God.

Historical Setting

The Twenty-third Psalm is so simple yet elegant, and so encouraging, that it has been a favorite of people in all sorts of locations and cultures. Part of the psalm's genius is that it contains nothing that limits it to a given time. Thus this timeless song of trust does not have a strict historical setting as such.

Of course, it can hardly have been composed before the name of the Lord (Hebrew *Yahweh*) was generally known (i.e., the fifteenth century B.C.; cf. Exodus 3:14–18) or, indeed, before David's time (he was king from 1011 B.C. to 971 B.C.). David was in all probability the author of the psalm, although this is not entirely provable from the superscription, "A Psalm of David." The ancient versions differ on the content of these superscriptions; some do not even number them among the verses of their psalms. Thus we have no way to be completely sure that this title "A Psalm of David" or any other title is original.

Form and Structure

Psalm 23 is a very carefully structured poem. Several elegant patterns are at work at the same time in this psalm.

First, note how "the LORD" is mentioned right at the beginning and at the end of the psalm, but not explicitly otherwise. Such a beginning–ending structure is typically called an *inclusio* and helps the careful hearer or reader appreciate that the focus—from beginning to end, as it were—is on God.

Next, note the transition of metaphors from verses 1–4 to verses 5–6. In verses 1–4 the speaker (that's you and I—not just David) compares himself or herself metaphorically to a sheep. But in verses 5–6 the speaker is a human, dining at God's table, worshiping at God's house. Thus, subtly and naturally so that it is hardly noticeable, we move from one sort of experience to another. In verses 1–4, God is the good protective shepherd. In verses 5–6, he is the good protective host—at whose "house" the worshiper is always joyously welcome.

Then look at verses 4–5 in the center of the psalm. Notice how they address God directly ("thou"), whereas God is referred to in the third person before and after those verses. Such a pattern is concentric: at the center is direct conversation, and surrounding that is direct testimonial.

Finally, note the rapid shift of scenes. We begin at the pasture (v. 2), then find ourselves at the water (v. 2). Then we are on the path (v. 3) and then in the dark valley (v. 4). Suddenly we are at the meal our host has prepared (v. 5). Our enemies are there, but they cannot harm us since our host has obviously chosen to protect and honor us. Finally, we see ourselves at the Lord's house (in one sense the tabernacle of ancient Israel; in a broader sense, wherever we worship; v. 6). What a beautiful tapestry of confidence in God!

Application

1. We need God's help and protection. It is foolish to think that simply by exercising our own judgment, by being generally intelligent and reliably informed, we can get through life on our own skills. We are indeed dependent on God to shepherd us and to welcome us into his care.
2. The sheep can trust the Shepherd. God is a good guide and leader, who desires the best for his flock. Life's dangers are not something God removes; the dark valleys and the enemies in our presence are real threats to us. But God sees to it that our confidence in him will not be misplaced.
3. God is with us wherever we are: on the road, like sheep on the move, exposed; or settled; or at God's house, symbolically "close" to him, in a worshipful and peaceful environment.
4. God is loyal. All our lives his loyalty may be counted on. In his loyalty he gives us not just the barest of necessities but spiritual prosperity of a most abundant sort (cf. Ephesians 3:20).

Chapter 15

PROVERBS 31:10–31
In Praise of Wives and Mothers

RSV   **Paraphrase**

31:10–12 A woman of quality is valuable for her own sake and for her husband's.

13–15 She is hardworking and well organized.

16–18 She is decisive, a good manager, strong, and energetic.

19–22 She is skilled and productive in making clothes for her family, and also generous to the needy.

23 Her husband is respected.

24–26 Some of the clothing she makes is so good it can be sold commercially. She is "clothed" with dignity, organization, and wisdom.

27 She is not lazy.

28–31 She is praised by her family and by others for her godliness.

Introduction

Women have enormous power to do good, in society and in their families—even in a so-called man's world. In ancient Israel women were almost always married once they reached marriage age, and they had no means of birth control. Therefore, this passage pays special attention to the role of a woman as both wife and mother. Its appeal has always consisted in its portrayal of a truly outstanding woman partly as a model for other women to compare themselves to and partly as a reminder of how much a godly woman means to her husband and family. Its special appeal in our own time relates to its portrayal of the godly woman as astute in business, decisive, and well-organized administratively.

Vocabulary

31:10	*good wife*	Better: high-quality wife, or wife of quality. The Hebrew term signifies distinction, not just goodness.
11	*heart*	Or: mind.
	gain	Literally: plunder. The gain is what she provides him, not what he himself makes.
13	*wool and flax*	Standard terms for some of the necessities of life (cf. Hosea 2:9), indicating therefore *all* the necessities.
14	*she brings . . . from afar*	She spares no energy to get what is needed, even if it is not easily available.
16	*the fruit of her hands*	Her earnings.
17	*makes her arms strong*	There is no reference to exercise here, but to her decision to make her arms do hard work.
18	*profitable*	Better: good, first-rate.
19	*distaff*	Better: spindle whorl, the little disk at the bottom of the spinning staff

		(spindle) that gives momentum to the spin.
21	*in scarlet*	The Greek Old Testament (Septuagint) and Latin Old Testament (Vulgate) translate the ambiguous Hebrew word here as "doubly," which is probably the more accurate translation (all her household are doubly clothed).
23	*in the gates*	Legal and official matters were conducted in the large open gateways of ancient cities. Her husband would be respected enough to have a role in such matters.
22	*purple*	Dyed wool.
24	*garments . . . girdles*	It is clear in the Hebrew that these indicate not so much full-scale manufacturing as the occasional production of a special piece. "Girdles" is better translated as sash, or sashes.
25	*laughs at*	Looks forward to, without worry (because she has provided for it).
26	*kindness*	Better: loyalty, faithfulness.
30	*vain*	Worthless, perishable.
31	*of the fruit of her hands*	The reward she has earned.
	in the gates	Where responsible people take note of what's happening (cf. v. 23).

Biblical Context

Throughout history, women have demonstrated managerial skills and have used those skills just as well as men could. The Bible contains many examples of women with the same sort of outstanding leadership, organizational, and motivational skills that are mentioned in Proverbs 31:10–31. For instance, we see Naomi, Ruth's mother-in-law, wisely arranging Ruth's affairs and initiating a complicated property transaction (Ruth 2:22; 3:1–4; 4:9–10). We see Deborah governing Israel in the days of the Judges and serving as general over the Israelite troops (Judges 4). We see queens like Bathsheba (1 Kings 1:11–31; 2:13–22), Jezebel (1 Kings 18–19; 21), and Athaliah (2 Kings 11) having a profound impact on affairs of state. We see Miriam, Moses' sister, as one of the three leaders of the exodus from Egypt (Micah 6:4). And so on.

In the New Testament church, women supported Jesus (Luke 8:2–3) and were among the apostles (Romans 16:7 [Junias is clearly a woman's name]) and ministers (Philippians 4:2–3).

It has often been suggested that Proverbs 31:10–31 is one of the parts of the Bible written by a woman. This is indeed quite possible. But the fact that in our English versions it follows 31:1–9, a section definitely written by a woman (31:1), cannot be taken as evidence for this, since the Greek Old Testament (Septuagint), for example, places our passage several chapters apart from the poem, in 31:1–9.

Historical Setting

This section of Proverbs cannot be dated specifically. A precise dating would not matter anyway, since the topic is more or less timeless in its relevance.

The passage does assume what was virtually always true in ancient times—that adult women married and had children. It also assumes that industry was of the cottage type. Men and women did not go off to work in factories or business centers. They worked out of their homes. Moreover, a woman's "household" (vs. 15, 21, 27) was not just her husband and children. Grandparents, son's wives (and grandchildren), and servants (v. 15) were also part of the household. Thus the woman described in our passage is managing the equivalent of a small business.

And she *is* a businesswoman, a true manager. She manufactures (vs. 13, 18, 22, 24) and sells (v. 24). She buys property (v. 16). She assigns jobs to workers and supervises them (v. 15). She manages a variety of agricultural involvements (vs. 13, 16, 19a). She makes a profit (v. 11) and gives to charity out of that profit (v. 20). She also teaches and advises (v. 26) and is appreciated socially (v. 31). She is good at planning (vs. 21, 25) and is trustworthy (v. 11). She is resourceful (v. 14) and aware of the needs and concerns of others (vs. 12, 15, 23, 27). In return, she knows what it is to be loved and appreciated (vs. 11, 28–31).

Ancient Israel was, culturally, much more of a man's world than is, for example, modern America. The fact that even in that society godly people were instructed to recognize the significant power and responsibility of the wife and mother should instruct us as well.

In ancient Israel, by the way, people didn't marry for love in the same way we think of it. Their marriages were almost always arranged before they even reached puberty, by their parents, as is still the case in much of the world today. Accordingly, sheer physical attraction is not an important factor in this woman's acceptance by her husband or friends. What makes her special is not beauty but how beautifully she reflects godliness (v. 30). Good looks, on which modern people spend billions of dollars a year, are simply not important to God.

Form and Structure

This passage is a special type of poem, called an acrostic. An acrostic poem starts each new verse with a new letter of the alphabet. There are twenty-two verses in this poem, because there are twenty-two letters in the Hebrew alphabet. Remember the old song, "Mother"? "M is for the many things you gave me. O means only . . ." etc. That's an acrostic too. By going through the alphabet, the poet says in effect that a good wife and mother is a wonderful thing, from A to Z.

The alphabetical arrangement of the Hebrew poem means that the hearers or readers of the original Hebrew noticed a structure that just isn't noticeable in English. Thus the poem may seem to hop from subject to subject in different verses, but it really is carefully planned and unified.

Some typical Hebrew exaggerations are used in the poem. For example, we are told in verse 18 that this outstanding woman's "lamp does not go out at night," as if she never slept. Or in verse 29 her family tells her "you surpass them all" (all other women). These exaggerations are called hyperbole, which is purposeful exaggeration in order to get a point across. What those statements actually mean is that the woman of quality is not so self-centered that she refuses to work on into the night when it is necessary (v. 18) and that her family can't imagine themselves having a better wife and mother (v. 29).

Application

1. A woman of quality is a skillful leader, manager, and organizer.
2. She is also a hard worker.
3. She cares well for those people and things which are her responsibility.
4. She need not be good-looking to attract praise and love.

Chapter 16

ISAIAH 35
"The Eyes of the Blind Shall Be Opened"

RSV	Paraphrase
35:1–2	Barren areas will suddenly break out with flowers and joyful music, becoming like areas famed for their lushness, when they see the Lord arrive gloriously.
3–4	People discouraged and afraid should take heart; God is coming to set things right and to rescue his people.
5–7	Frailties and imperfections such as blindness, deafness, or being crippled or unable to speak will all be healed. Previously parched, scorched areas will suddenly have abundant water and wetlands.
8–10	There will be a highway through the former barren wilderness, safe and direct for the use of God's redeemed people to come home with joy and freedom to the new Jerusalem.

Introduction

The hope and joy expressed in this passage have always been an inspiration to Bible readers. No matter how bleak the present situation may be, God's arrival on the scene will produce a dramatic reversal.

The new age in Christ, longed for by Isaiah and the other prophets, is yet to be *eternally* established. Therefore it is an object of hope among contemporary Christians everywhere. We, too, await the dramatic changes that God will bring about at the end of the age, and look forward to walking with all the redeemed on the "Holy Way" to the heavenly Jerusalem.

Vocabulary

35:2	*glory of Lebanon*	Lebanon was the most densely forested and flowered part of ancient Palestine (cf. Hosea 14:6–7). Its "glory" was its lovely vegetation.
	Carmel and Sharon	Two lush regions: Carmel is a promontory on the northwest coast of Israel; Sharon is the low coastal Mediterranean plain.
4	*vengeance*	Better: righteous intervention.
6	*hart*	Male deer.
7	*haunt of jackals*	Where jackals gather; a wild, desolate area.
8	*highway*	A main roadway.
	unclean	Persons not holy (religiously rather than physically unclean).
	fools . . . err therein	Even people of limited intelligence will not wander off the road.
9	*ravenous beast*	Dangerous wild animal looking for prey.
10	*ransomed*	People "bought back," belonging to God once again.

Zion	A poetic name for the Jerusalem of the coming age, derived from the name of the mountain on which the city was located (see also Revelation 21:10 to 22:5).
upon their heads	Like a crown.

Biblical Context

Note the contrast to Isaiah 34. There we find a graphic description of judgment against evil in the world order, personified by Israel's archenemy Edom. By contrast, chapter 35 depicts the new order of peace, righteousness, and "coming home."

The coming of the Messiah, Jesus, was the initial part of the fulfillment of this prophetic text. In Matthew 11:4–5 (likewise Luke 7:22) Jesus confirms to the disciples of John the Baptist that he is indeed the Messiah by citing miracles he had performed (the blind receiving sight, etc.) as evidence that the long-awaited era had begun to dawn. That era is, of course, still to be completed, as Jesus told his disciples, or as Hebrews 12:12, citing Isaiah 35:3, also confirms; we need to strengthen our weak hands and feeble knees in spite of the present hardships, because the full blessings of eternal life and the "new heaven and new earth" (Revelation 21:1) have not yet arrived.

Historical Setting

Although they have brought hope to all ages, these words were first spoken to bring comfort and encouragement to a generation of Israelites who saw only distress and hardship ahead. Sometime during Isaiah's years as a prophet (about 740–690 B.C.) he was inspired to compose this chapter. Those years saw the power of a rather brutal imperialistic nation, Assyria, increase steadily. In 733, Assyria annexed most of the Northern Kingdom of Israel. In 722, Assyria captured all of the north and exiled many thousands of its people to various foreign places (see 2 Kings 17). By 701, all of the Southern Kingdom of Judah was in the hands of invading Assyrians except Jerusalem, which was miraculously spared (Isaiah 37).

Eventually, as Isaiah also predicted, the people of Judah would be exiled to foreign lands, almost never again to know true independence but always to live under the domination of other peoples. In chapter 35, however, the promise that all who were faithful would one day see God's deliverance is sung in hope. The passage describes God's redeeming his people in dramatic language that goes far beyond describing mere political deliverance. It is obvious that Isaiah intends his audience—and that includes us—to see in these words a description of the dawning of a new age yet to come, an age of eternal reward.

Form and Structure

Isaiah 35 is a poem, of the sort that predicts what are often called restoration blessings. The restoration is the period when God intervenes to restore the fortunes of his people. Restoration may, of course, happen in our individual lives from time to time and in the collective lives of God's people at different times. But the final restoration, in all its grandeur, is what is being talked about here.

Note the many reversals. Barrenness is reversed into fruitfulness (vs. 1–2), dry desert to wetlands (vs. 6–7), weakness to strength (v. 3), fear to confidence (v. 4), infirmity to health (vs. 5–6), unpassable wasteland to a highway (v. 8), danger to safety (v. 9). The result: terrific joy for all God's people (v. 10).

Note also the theme of serendipity (surprise happiness). Happiness is the keynote of the chapter. Even inanimate things like deserts are glad and sing for joy (v. 1) when they see God's glory finally manifest (v. 2).

Naturally, much of the passage is symbolically suggestive, exaggerated for effect (hyperbole). But that doesn't detract from its impact; on the contrary, it enhances it. Here is real rejoicing, talked about in a grand way, in which the happiness we will all one day know in Christ in our eternal reward is described in earthly terms that give the impression of joy all around. Everything will be changed, everything made new. The old will have finally "passed away" (2 Corinthians 5:17).

Application

1. Present temporary hardships will one day yield to great, continuing joy.
2. Realistic hope of the future encourages diligence now (Isaiah 35:3–4).
3. To be redeemed by God is to be happy indeed.

Chapter 17

JEREMIAH 1
Jeremiah's Call to Be a Prophet

RSV	Paraphrase
1:1–3	Identification of the author of the book, Jeremiah, and the years that he served as a prophet under three Judean kings, 628–587 B.C.
4–5	God announces to Jeremiah that he was always intended to be a prophet.
6–8	Jeremiah protests that he is too young, but God insists and reassures Jeremiah that he will protect him.
9–10	God symbolically "touches" Jeremiah's mouth, as a way of commissioning that mouth to speak about such things as great changes in the status of nations.
11–12	God causes Jeremiah to see a vision, one word of which is to remind him that God will carry out the words that he will announce through Jeremiah.

13–16   In a second vision, Jeremiah sees that a great invasion and conquest is coming against Judah. This is because Judah has disobeyed God's laws, including the laws against polytheism and idolatry (the first two commandments).

17–19   God again instructs Jeremiah to speak boldly the words he receives. God tells him that every sort of person will resent and oppose him, but that he must and will carry on, with God's help.

Introduction

Poor Jeremiah. God calls him to announce a message of doom and disaster, with the assurance that most of those who hear that message will resent it and will do their best to make Jeremiah's life miserable. What young man or woman would want to enter the ministry if he or she could be guaranteed to encounter virtually nothing but trouble?

Loneliness, rejection, bitter opposition, official retaliation, the conquest of his homeland—all these and more were to be Jeremiah's lot. God had called him to be a prophet, and carrying out that call would involve him in such troubles. But he *was* called by God, and he *was* willing. And God promised to be with him—not to make carrying out his calling easy but, rather, possible.

Vocabulary

1:1	*of the priests*	Jeremiah was from a priest's family—a descendant of Aaron.
	Anathoth	A city about three miles north of Jerusalem, where many priests lived.
2	*thirteenth year of his reign*	528 B.C.
3	*eleventh year of Zedekiah*	597 B.C.

	captivity of *Jerusalem*	Its capture and the deportation of its population in 597 B.C. by the Babylonians.
5	*consecrated you*	Set you aside, specially designated you.
	the nations	Various nations of the world, not just Judah.
6	*how to speak*	A protest of exaggerated humility, meaning, in effect: I am not a skilled orator.
8	*deliver*	Rescue, save from death.
9	*put forth his* *hand*	See below, Biblical Context.
10	*over nations and* *over kingdoms*	I.e., Jeremiah was to prophesy even about the destinies of nations.
11	*rod of almond*	Branch from an almond tree.
12	*watching*	The Hebrew word for "branch from an almond tree" is almost the same as the word for "watching."
14	*evil*	Harm, trouble, disaster, not necessarily moral evil.
15	*lo*	Here is the situation.
	tribes	People groups.
	set . . . throne *. . . gates*	Kings did this as a sign that they had conquered a city.
	against . . . *against*	These prepositions go with the verb "come" (come . . . against . . .) and do not relate to the thrones being set up.
16	*burned incense*	A mistranslation. The Hebrew word means to burn (offerings), to worship.

	the works of their own hands	Idols. This is a common way of describing how unimportant idols should be regarded.
17	*gird up your loins*	An expression meaning: get ready for action. It comes from the practice of tying one's robe around one's waist so as not to be slowed down in running or fighting.
	dismayed	Scared, discouraged.
18	*fortified city . . . bronze walls*	Symbolic language for: tough, able to withstand.

Biblical Context

Only false prophets could actually choose the prophetic profession. True prophets had it chosen for them. They were called by God to be his representatives, and refusing the call could have unpleasant results (Jonah 1–2). God does much of his work in the world through people rather than directly. He only sometimes speaks for himself, as it were.

This chapter describes Jeremiah's call to speak for God. He knew he was called because God both spoke to him (v. 4, etc.) and appeared to him (v. 9). A young man (v. 6), he learned that God had had this responsibility in mind for him all along (v. 5). Other prophets were called in similar ways. Amos, for example, was called later in life, out of an established career, without any "training for the ministry" (Amos 7:14–15) but by the direct word of God. Isaiah was called while worshiping in the temple. His call, like Jeremiah's, involved God's speaking to him and showing him visions, but of a somewhat different kind (Isaiah 6). Ezekiel was called by a grand, complex vision of God arriving suddenly on an omnidirectional chariot and by "commissioning" language similar to Jeremiah's and Isaiah's (Ezekiel 1–3).

The fact that Jeremiah was to encounter plenty of opposition (Jeremiah 1:19; cf. vs. 8, 17) was not really a new thing. Prophets from Moses to John the Baptist lived with opposition on a regular basis. People are never very likely to rejoice at having their sins pointed out to them or to accept easily the kind of devoted, unselfish life-style that God knows is best for them.

Did Jeremiah really see and feel God's hand (v. 9)? Yes, but not exactly in the way that we would see or feel another person's hand. No human has ever truly seen God, because God is not visible (1 John 4:12). However, God has sometimes "appeared" to people in such a way that they were caused to see *something*—a shape, a part of a "body," an outline, or the like that they knew represented God. They were allowed to see or feel enough to let them know that God was present, but they could not in fact see what God looked like, because from the point of view of human perception God does not "look like" anything. (For some examples of visions of God, see Exodus 33:23; Isaiah 6:1; Ezekiel 1:26–27; Daniel 7:9.)

Historical Setting

In 628 B.C. when Jeremiah was called to be a prophet, the good reforms of King Josiah, which helped Judah temporarily to return to a more godly society, had not yet occurred. (They would come in about six years, partly as a result of Jeremiah's preaching.) The same basic violations of God's law (Jeremiah 1:16) that had caused God to allow the north, Israel, to be destroyed by the Assyrians almost a hundred years earlier (2 Kings 17) were now rampant in the south, Judah.

Jeremiah was called to preach during Judah's last days. Zedekiah (Jeremiah 1:3), Judah's last king before the conquest by the Babylonians, was to be particularly fierce in harassing Jeremiah (chapter 37) and might have killed him if he thought he could get away with it. So doom was coming, and doom is what Jeremiah had to preach. It was a hard time to be a prophet—but was there ever an easy time?

Form and Structure

In Jeremiah 1:5, God says that he has predestined or foreordained Jeremiah to be a prophet. We can understand that easily enough. God can plan for any child, born to any parents, to have certain benefits, opportunities, or responsibilities. And we also know that Jeremiah could have rejected God's foreordaining, just as any of us can reject God and his will for our lives—though, of course, at great price.

The wording "Before I formed you in the womb I knew you" is, however, troublesome to many people, because it seems to say that before Jeremiah was even conceived, he was a knowable entity—as sperm or something. But that is not the meaning here at all. The Hebrew verb for "know" has in the Old Testament a very wide range of meanings: imagine, think, foreknow, recognize. Moreover, because the verse is poetic in form, we must not separate the three statements from one another. The poetry is of a type called synonymous, and all three parts are meant to be taken together. Thus knew and consecrated and appointed all are getting at the same thing, not different things: Jeremiah's career has been long planned by God. Beyond that the verse says nothing at all about predestination in general, or Jeremiah's predestination to heaven or hell, or anything of the sort.

There are two visions in this passage. Visions are often God's visual aids. They do not exist for their own sake but as means of helping a message from God be memorable. In the first vision, Jeremiah is vividly taught that God will be *watching* his word because of the way the vision is worded. In the second, he is reminded of how *explosive* the times are by seeing a pot about to boil over. These visions help Jeremiah understand what God is saying to him, but they have no other special value or symbolism.

Application

1. Obeying God does not provide an easy life.
2. Speaking God's truth does not guarantee a warm reception.
3. What God determines to do, he will carry out.

Chapter 18

DANIEL 5
The Handwriting on the Wall

RSV	Paraphrase
5:1–4	The king of Babylon, Belshazzar, uses holy cups and pitchers from the temple of the Lord as drinking vessels for his idolatrous feast.
5–9	A detached hand writes on the walls. Terrified, the king calls for specialists, offering an enormous reward for the correct interpretation of what the hand wrote. But no one can figure out what the letters mean.
10–12	The queen mother suggests that Daniel could interpret the writing, because of his God-given insight.
13–16	The king offers Daniel the great reward if he can interpret the writing.
17–23	Before interpreting what the hand wrote, Daniel reminds the king that his grandfather, the great Nebuchadnezzar, was punished by God for his arrogance and that King Belshazzar has been acting just like his grandfather.

24–31   David interprets the writing. It turns out to be a cryptic prediction of doom for Belshazzar and his kingdom. God fulfills the prediction. Belshazzar dies, and his kingdom falls to the Persians.

Introduction

From this passage comes the expression "the handwriting on the wall," referring to an indication of one's coming fate. The chapter describes the sudden end of a great dynasty and a great empire, because the kings of that dynasty and empire thought they could get away with paying no heed to the true God, arrogating to themselves undue pride and power. It also shows us one old man through whom God was at work, able to do what teams of experts found impossible, because God was with him and not with them.

This story is written in Aramaic, a language similar to Hebrew roughly as French is similar to Spanish. Aramaic was the international common language of Daniel's day, and Daniel 2:4 to 7:28 is composed in it. The rest of the book of Daniel is in Hebrew.

Vocabulary

5:1	*in front of*	In the presence of, along with.
2	*when he tasted*	Partly under the influence of. "Tasted" means virtually "drunk plenty" in this idiomatic expression.
	his father	Nebuchadnezzar was probably Belshazzar's grandfather, but "father" can refer to any ancestor in Aramaic.
	wives, concubines	Two words for different classes of women who served the king or were part of his harem. Not queens. Also in verse 23.
5	*fingers of a man's hand*	A detached hand, not just the fingers, as the end of the verse confirms.

	opposite the lampstand	There would have been many lampstands in the room. "The" here means a certain. The point is that the area was well lighted.
6	*color changed*	He went pale.
	his limbs gave way	He felt weak.
7	*Chaldeans*	A particular class of wise men from the king's own ethnic group, also called the Chaldeans.
	reads	Pronounces meaningfully. The message was in Aramaic, language that indicated no vowels in writing and required comprehension to be read.
	purple . . . chain of gold	Signs of royal authority.
	the third ruler	See below, Historical Setting.
8	*wise men*	Not a new group, but a summarizing term for the enchanters, etc., mentioned in verse 7.
10	*queen*	Almost certainly the queen mother, who often enjoyed a superior status to any of the king's wives.
	"live for ever!"	Standard words of greeting (cf. 6:6; 21) akin to "Long live the king!" They have nothing to do with a wish for eternal life.
11	*holy gods*	Probably plural, because the queen mother was a typical polytheist, but the form in Aramaic can have a singular meaning when applied to God. Thus possible: holy God. (Also in v. 14.)

12	*excellent spirit*	Not "very good attitude" but: outstanding spiritual power, or the like.
	Belteshazzar	Daniel's Babylonian name (1:7), which meant "Guard the king's life."
	show	Explain, make known.
15	*the wise men, the enchanters*	This means "the wise men, the enchanters, etc." (Cf. vs. 7,8.)
17	*Let your gifts . . . another*	This was not meant literally. See below, Historical Setting.
19	*all*	All sorts of—a standard idiom.
	put down	Removed from power, impoverished, imprisoned, or such things.
20	*glory*	Honor, prestige, etc.
21	*beast*	Wild animal; not monster or anything similar.
	dew of heaven	The reference is simply to dew; "of. heaven" refers to the moisture source, the sky or air.
	Most High God	A term for God in the book of Daniel.
23	*whose are all your ways*	Who controls as he wills your whole life.
25	MENE, TEKEL, PARSIN	The vowels we read in English are from the Middle Ages. The Aramaic words were spelled without vowels: *mn', tkl, prs*. (The N on PARSIN is a· mistake that crept into later texts of the book of Daniel but was not present originally.) These words constitute a cryptogram. *mn'* can mean *mina* (a unit of money weighing about sixty shekels, or two pounds). *tkl* is Aramaic for shekel, a half-ounce weight or coin. *prs* can stand for

peras, a half mina. So some of those who saw the handwriting probably thought it mentioned the names of coins or weights, like dollar, dime, nickel or ton, pound, ounce, but could not see what revelatory significance— interpretation—such words could possibly have. Daniel, of course, read them differently, as verbs, with the prophetic insight God provided him.

26	MENE	Aramaic *mn'* if taken as a verb means to count or number.
27	TEKEL	Aramaic *tkl* as a verb means to weigh.
28	PERES	Aramaic *prs* as a verb means to divide, and as a noun can also suggest "Persia."
30	*That very night*	This sounds dramatic but is misleading. In the Aramaic it may mean nothing more than "One night" or "During the night." The death of Belshazzar thus could have come later than the night of the banquet.
31	*Darius the Mede*	A complicated identification. See below, Historical Setting.

Biblical Context

The book of Daniel describes in part the adventures of Daniel and his associates Shadrach, Meshach, and Abednego (see chapter 3 especially for the latter three). Chapters 1–6 are mostly about how God helped them to remain faithful to him and showed himself superior to the "gods" of the Babylonians and Persians.

Thereafter, in chapters 7–12, the book concentrates on visions Daniel had that allow him—and readers of the book—to get a sense of how history would develop in terms of some of the Near Eastern nations. By the time that Belshazzar was king, Daniel was an old man, having been forcibly deported as a child to Babylon by the great Nebuchadnezzar about 597 B.C. (cf. 2 Kings 24:10–16). Under

Nebuchadnezzar he became a wise man/prophet/adviser to the king, and an administrator. However, during the reigns of Nebuchadnezzar's immediate successors, Evil-merodach, Nergal-sharezer, and Belshazzar's father, Nabonidus, Daniel had been virtually in retirement as a prophetic wise man to the Babylonians. Thus he comes out of retirement at about age seventy here, forgotten by the king but remembered by the queen mother, who had seen him in action when she, too, was much younger.

Historical Setting

The story takes place in 539 B.C., the last year of the Babylonian Empire. Belshazzar was not an independent king in his own right, but with his father, Nabonidus, who had made him co-regent in 556 B.C. Belshazzar ruled in Babylon while his father went on military campaigns (for years at a time), mostly in Arabia. Belshazzar was killed by the invading Persians, whose king, Cyrus the Great, led them in the conquest of Babylon's former empire and beyond.

Daniel thus could be made only "third ruler" (Daniel 5:7) behind Nabonidus and Belshazzar. His apparent declining of this honor (v. 17) was in fact merely the so-called "false humility" or exaggerated deference that is common to Eastern cultures (cf. David's comparing himself to "a dead dog . . . a flea" in 1 Samuel 24:14). The king certainly would not have taken Daniel's deferential speech all that seriously. He knew that Daniel would not despise such gifts. Thus Daniel was indeed awarded the position (Daniel 5:29) for the short time that the empire had left. Such power was not entirely new to Daniel. He had held a major administrative position in the days of Nebuchadnezzar (2:48–49) and, later, climaxed his government as a head satrap (governor; see 6:2).

The identity of Darius the Mede, mentioned in 5:31, is often a subject of debate, since the only Darius to become king anywhere around the period in question was the Darius who reigned 522–486 B.C. and who was definitely not a Mede. The solution to this problem appears to lie in the fact that the Persian general Gubaru, who did take over the administration of Babylon on behalf of King Cyrus (while Cyrus continued to extend his empire), was popularly identified as "Darius." Gubaru was indeed a Mede, a citizen of Media, which was by this time a part of the Persian Empire.

Form and Structure

The chapter is a self-contained story, one of several such narratives in the book of Daniel. This happens to be the only story about Daniel and Belshazzar, though stories about Daniel and various Babylonian or Persian kings are central to the first half of the book.

Storytelling in ancient times was often highly stylized. That is, it employed certain typical vocabulary, sentence patterns, themes, repetitions. The stories in Daniel are often stylized, and chapter 5 is no exception. Note, for example, how Daniel, speaking in verses 23–24, uses many of the same expressions that the narrator uses in verses 2–4, though with considerable variations and substitutions. There are at least three possible reasons for this. One is that Daniel himself is the narrator. Another is that the narrator was inspired to convey the conversations of the king, the queen mother, and Daniel in terms that would most accurately communicate the essentials to his or her audience. Another is that the narrator shaped the narration partly according to what the king, the queen mother, and Daniel had actually said.

We do not know enough about how a book like Daniel was composed to decide among these options. What we can say, however, is that for all its simplicity of style and format, the story has always had a remarkable impact.

Application

1. God is sovereign—over the greatest king and the greatest empire.
2. What is sacred to God ought not to be trifled with (Daniel 5:2, 23), least of all in an arrogant manner.
3. One person with the wisdom of God is more valuable than many persons relying on their own wisdom, even if they might be experts from a human point of view.

Chapter 19

HOSEA 1:2 to 2:1
A Prophecy Through a Family

RSV	Paraphrase
1:2	Hosea's marriage and children to symbolize events in "the land."
3–5	Marriage concluded; first son's name symbolizes defeat at Jezreel.
6–7	Daughter's name symbolizes lack of pity on Israel, in contrast to Judah.
8–9	Second son's name symbolizes God's rejection of Israel.
10–11, 2:1	New situation to come: an eventual end to the miseries previously predicted; new names (or meanings of names) for the children.

Introduction

Here is a story of how a prophet's marriage and the unusual names he is told to give to his children function as memory aids for the message God is giving to the people of Israel. Much confusion has surrounded this story, particularly since a misreading of verse 2 can lead—as it often has—to the conclusion that Hosea actually was commanded by God to marry a prostitute. Nevertheless, Bible readers have always been fascinated by this marriage that symbolizes a prophetic message and by these children given negative, then later positive, names.

Vocabulary

1:2   *wife of harlotry*   The Hebrew here does not mean a wife who is a harlot. The word "harlotry" is in the abstract in the original language, signifying a characteristic of the wife that Hosea will marry but not saying anything at all about her profession. A translation "woman tainted by harlotry" would be accurate.

children of harlotry   Again, the language cannot mean children born of a harlot or children who will become harlots but, rather, children affected by harlotry, or the like.

the land commits great harlotry   Here we can see clearly that God, in speaking to Hosea, is using the term "harlotry" in a metaphorical sense. We have seen that a metaphor is a comparison that does not use a comparative word such as "like" or "as." Hosea, like several of the other Old Testament prophets, uses adultery and harlotry as metaphors for Israel's religious infidelity (e.g., 4:10, 12, 18; 5:3, 4; 6:10; 7:4; 9:1). After all, who is more promiscuous than a prostitute? Thus people who are religiously promiscuous—that is, who worship many gods other than Yahweh—can be compared metaphorically to people who engage in "harlotry."

4 *the blood of Jezreel*   This refers to the bloody massacre of both northern and southern royalty in 842 B.C. by the usurper Jehu (2 Kings 10), who was the founder of the "house [dynasty] of Jehu," the dynasty of which Jeroboam II, the king of Israel when Hosea and Gomer were having their children, was the last occupant.

5 *break the bow*   To defeat militarily.

valley of Jezreel   A broad fertile plain stretching for miles through northern Israel, the scene of many great military battles in Israel's history. From this plain rises prominently Mt. Megiddo (Hebrew *har megiddo,* Greek *Armageddon*), which already in Old Testament times symbolized the site of decisive warfare involving God's people. In Revelation 16:16 the term Armageddon has this same symbolism.

6 *house of Israel*   The family of Israel, the Israelite people.

8 *weaned*   Children were not weaned until about age three in Old Testament times, so there is a substantial space between the second and the third child.

9 *not your God*   In the Hebrew, these words recall the revelation of God's name Yahweh to Moses in Exodus 3:14 and can thus mean "I am not your I AM." (Yahweh is a third-person form closely related to the first-person "I AM.") When God first made Israel his people, he gave them his name. Now, by taking his name from them, he is also declaring them not to be his people any longer. The name of the third child emphasizes this, of course.

10 *Sons*

Children. The Hebrew term is not limited to male children.

the living God

People in ancient times worshiped many "gods," all of whom were mere dead idols. Yahweh alone was really alive. Similarly in the New Testament (e.g., Romans 16:27) he is called "the only wise God"; that is, the only God who actually has intelligence. Other "gods" are merely dumb sculptures.

11 *gathered together*

Israel (in the north) and Judah (in the south) had been politically and religiously divided since 931 B.C. (1 Kings 11–12). This predicts their reunification—especially religiously.

one head

The reunification of God's people under a great, true, eternal new David (the one head) is a major hope of the Old Testament prophets (Isaiah 9:7; Ezekiel 37:24; Hosea 3:5; Amos 9:11; etc.).

up from the land

Probably this refers to returning from the land of exile, but it could mean up from the underworld, or back from death, i.e., revival as a people.

Jezreel

The first child's name now used again symbolically but in a positive sense. The name literally means in Hebrew "God plants" and has the connotation here of rich agricultural blessing or great abundance in general.

| 2:1 | *"My people"* | A positive name change for the second son (see 1:8). |
| | *"She has obtained pity"* | A positive name change for the daughter. In the Hebrew this new name is simply Not Pitied (see 1:6) with the "Not" removed. In English, Pitied sounds rather sad, so the RSV translators chose the longer wording for the positive name. Shown Compassion or Favored would be possible alternative English renderings of this name. |

Biblical Context

The Old Testament prophets were not really original in what they said. They were often quite creative in how they said it, but their basic message was an old one, the same message that God had revealed to Israel through Moses. The prophets were called by God especially to announce the impending fulfillment of two kinds of things: covenant punishments and covenant blessings. The covenant (Law), made with Israel and recorded in the books of Exodus, Leviticus, Numbers, and Deuteronomy, provided for punishments if Israel disobeyed God's law and blessings if it obeyed. It also provided for "restoration" blessings—blessings God would give by sheer dint of his grace after the people had sinned against him and had been punished as a nation. Deuteronomy 4:21–31 provides a brief outline of Israel's history as predicted through Moses to Israel: a period of blessings (conquest and occupation of the Promised Land), followed by a period of punishment once the nation's sins had become too great to ignore (defeat, rejection, and exile), followed by an indefinite period of restoration blessing (the restoration and "new age"). Leviticus 26 and Deuteronomy 28–32 contain this basic chronological perspective on blessings and punishments in much greater detail.

Hosea, like all other orthodox prophets, was an announcer of these blessings and punishments. In his time the conquest and occupation of the Promised Land were ending, so his announcing concerned exclusively the coming period of punishment and the following era of restoration blessing. This is exactly what Hosea reveals via his marriage and the names of his children. The nation of Israel was so full of "prostitution"—unfaithfulness to God—that virtually *any* woman he married would have been affected or tainted by idolatry, willful sinfulness, economic injustice, distorted values, or the like. Merely by getting married, he could be said to be marrying a "wife of harlotry."

And merely having children would be to produce "children of harlotry"; that is, children who would be born into a society thoroughly tainted by such things, so complete was the corruption and degeneration of Israel in Hosea's day. The whole land was fully involved in this "harlotry" (1:2). Therefore, the result, as the Mosaic Law specified, had to be punishment.

One type of punishment specified for disobedience to God's covenant was defeat in war (Leviticus 26:17, 37; Deuteronomy 28:25, 49-52; etc.). That is what Jezreel's name symbolized, with its reference to the Jezreel massacre (2 Kings 10). Another type of punishment is anger and hostility instead of mercy and compassion (Leviticus 26:24, 41; Deuteronomy 28:28; etc.). Not Pitied's name symbolizes that. A closely related punishment is rejection as a people (Deuteronomy 29:27; 31:17; 32:30; etc.), symbolized by the name Not My People.

The three children had no prophetic role except through their names. Yet that was effective enough. Every time Hosea introduced his children, their names would occasion an opportunity to warn Israelites of the coming punishments!

But God's message to Israel through Hosea was not all negative. The "Yet" of Hosea 1:10 is very important. The period of punishment would eventually end. The fact that it would end is implicit here though explicit elsewhere in Hosea, e.g., 6:1–3; 14:4–8. After it would come the restoration, in which the earlier punishments would be compensated for. The name changes (or, in the case of Jezreel, a change in the perceived meaning of his name) in 1:11 to 2:1 signify that new era.

A note on chapter 3: The message of this chapter is virtually the same. Israel's sinfulness requires punishment (3:4), which will be followed by restoration (3:5). No children are mentioned here, but there is a marriage—to an adulteress, a woman who actually, literally has committed adultery. But this is a *different* marriage. Hosea never consummates it. The end of verse 3 says, literally, that "you shall not play the harlot, or belong to another man; so will I also be to you." In other words, this (second) wife symbolizes Israel

restrained and chastened (3:4), a sinful woman now forcibly restrained from infidelity. Thus, although chapter 3 closely parallels
chapter 1, it does not describe the same marriage.

Historical Setting

These events took place about 760–753 B.C., the last several years
of the reign of King Jeroboam II (793–753 B.C.). It is not possible to
tell exactly how many years elapsed between Hosea's receiving
from God his command to marry (1:2) and the birth of the last child
(1:8). A figure of about seven years cannot be too far from the mark.

These were days of prosperity and complacency in (northern)
Israel. Powerful nations usually hostile to Israel, such as Assyria
and Egypt, were not a threat, preoccupied as they were with other
problems and foes. Syria, Israel's nearest major enemy, had been
subdued by Jereboam II (2 Kings 14:25–28). Judah and Israel, often
at war in the past, were now at peace. So military troubles were few.
But religiously, the nation was sick and dying. Idolatry was rampant
(Hosea 2:13; 4:12–13; 8:4; etc.; cf. 2 Kings 14:24), Yahweh's
covenant was being ignored (Hosea 4:1–2), and the fertility god Baal
was occupying a far more prominent place in the public conscious-
ness than was Yahweh (2:8, 13; 7:16).

The fertility religion of Baal worship was popular partly because
it appealed to selfish motives. Baal religion did not emphasize either
personal or social ethics. It allowed people to do whatever they
wanted, no matter how self-centered or cruel to others, so long as
they faithfully brought ample sacrifices to the (many, conveniently
located) Baal shrines. According to this religion, Baal operated on a
tit-for-tat basis. He would give rain (his specialty) in the right
amounts, so that agriculture (the only significant employment of
these times) would prosper, as long as his worshipers gave him (and
his priests) plenty to eat—that is, sacrifices. Moreover, a worshiper
could have the confidence that Baal really accepted his or her
sacrifices because Baal was considered truly present at the shrines
by reason of his representative idol. (See the commentary on
Genesis 1 in chapter 1 of this book for more about idols or images.)
Finally, since sex was observed by the ancients to be the source of
'productivity'' in animal and human life, Baal religion believed that
ritual sex with a cult prostitute (4:14) on the part of worshipers
would stimulate Baal to have his own heavenly sex, from which the

procreation of all nature would flow. Sexual worship was, as you can imagine, quite popular with some people.

Compared to this, orthodox belief in an invisible Yahweh who strictly demanded justice and righteousness via his covenant, and whose worship required self-sacrifice and allowed no carnal self-indulgence, was just plain dull, restrictive, and old-fashioned.

Thus since its early days in the Promised Land in the time of the Judges, Israel had turned from Yahweh and largely ignored his law. After the split of the kingdom upon the death of Solomon (1 Kings 11), the north had established its own counterreligion featuring the idolatry of the "golden calves" at Dan and at Bethel. More cosmopolitan than Judah, Israel had also imported many of the religious beliefs and practices of its neighbors (e.g., 1 Kings 16:25–33). Centuries of dishonest business practices, crime, abuse of the poor and needy, religious unfaithfulness, distorted values, and so forth had finally made necessary the enforcement of the covenant warnings God had given through Moses to Israel (see above, Biblical Context). He was about to reject his people, see them destroyed in war, and remove his long-patient pity from them. In just two more decades (734 B.C.), the Assyrians would rise again and by force annex much of Israel (2 Kings 16; Isaiah 9:1–2; Hosea 5:8–10). In just three decades (722 B.C.), all of the Northern Kingdom would be conquered by the Assyrians and much of its population deported to Assyria (2 Kings 17). God's word through Hosea would indeed be carried out.

Form and Structure

The passage is a prophetic narrative centering on names. Names in ancient Israel were almost always positive. The only negative names we know of, in fact, are essentially prophetic: the name Ichabod, meaning Non-glory, announced Israel's defeat before the Philistines (1 Samuel 4:21). Isaiah's son Maher-shalal-hashbaz (Hasten spoil, hurry prey) and Hosea's children are among the few bearing such names.

Naming per se was considered a very important process in ancient times. The appropriate name for a child was an important concern. Thus, people did not choose names for their children before birth. Instead, they waited to select names suggested to them by events or conversations that occurred while the child was being born (see, for

example, Genesis 21:3–6; 25:25–26; 30:10–11). For God to announce
to Hosea his children's names is quite unusual, and the linking of
names to future events is also unusual. These names are, to put it
mildly, out of the ordinary pattern.

Our passage describes how actions (marrying a typical Israelite
woman, naming children) function to help convey a prophetic
message. We call it an enactment prophecy. The most famous of
these is probably Isaiah's going naked to symbolize the coming exile
of north Africans by the Assyrians. ("Exile" and "naked" are
virtually the same word in Hebrew, so the message was suggested
by the enactment.) For other examples of enactment prophecies, see
1 Kings 22:11; 2 Kings 13:15–19; Jeremiah 32:6–15.

Application

1. God cannot be disobeyed forever. Eventually, his covenant
   obligations demand that he enforce his law against people or
   nations with whom he has been patient long enough.
2. God's wrath is never an end in itself. Though God must some
   times exercise his wrath, his ultimate desire is restoration and
   blessing for his people.
3. Fidelity is very important in our relationship to God. We cannot
   truly say that we love him simply because we worship regularly,
   if we in fact are engaged in a "harlotry" of divided loyalties. Baal
   religion was a materialistic system that caused God to reject his
   people. Today his people are no less guilty if selfish materialism
   prevents them from being faithful to God (Matthew 7:19–24).

Chapter 20

MICAH 6:1–8
"Walk Humbly with Your God"

RSV	Paraphrase
6:1–2	The Lord launches a divine legal proceeding against Israel, with the mountains as a symbolic jury.
3–4	God declares his innocence. Their sin certainly cannot be blamed on him—he rescued, helped, and guided them.
5	Israel should reflect on its early history: how the king of Moab tried to get the false prophet Balaam to curse Israel and how Balaam ended up blessing them, or how God led Israel through the Jordan dry-shod, from one side (Shittim) to the other (Gilgal).
6–7	What then does God want from his people? Are sacrifices all he wants? Would even sacrificing one's oldest child be adequate to cover one's sins?
8	God has already told you what he wants: justice, loyalty to his covenant, and careful living.

Introduction

Is it possible for people to misunderstand what God really wants from them? To devote themselves to religious procedures without being truly religious? Absolutely. Micah, like his contemporaries Amos (Amos 5:21–22) and Hosea (Hosea 6:6), warned God's people that the formal aspect of religion, worshiping by offering sacrifices to God, was simply not enough. What God wants is not merely ritual but a life of obedience—walking "humbly with your God."

Vocabulary

6:1	*plead your case*	Defend yourself, if you can, against the charges the Lord is bringing.
2	*controversy*	Lawsuit or legal case.
	contend with Israel	Take Israel to court.
4	*house of bondage*	The situation of slavery.
	sent before you	Gave you the leadership of.
6	*come before*	Come to worship.
	burnt offerings	Animal meat offerings which were burned entirely as a gift to God. Worshipers ate part of other offerings, but not burnt offerings.
	calves a year old	Proper sacrificial animals at the right age (Leviticus 9:3).
7	*rams*	Common sacrificial animals (Leviticus 5:15).
	oil	A common sacrificial substance (Leviticus 2:4).
	transgression	Disobedience to God's law; sin.
	fruit of my body	My child.
	sin of my soul	My own sin.

8   *kindness*   Better: loyalty, faithfulness.

   humbly   Better: carefully, properly.

Biblical Context

The prophets were often led to call their audiences to reflect on the past and learn from it. At the heart of this passage are verses 3–5, which remind Israel of what God did for them. Had God wearied them—tired them out—by the demands he put upon them? Just the opposite! He has always generously protected them and paved the way for them. Have they forgotten that they started out as slaves in Egypt and would still be there if not for God's miraculous rescue (v. 4)? Have they forgotten that he led them for forty years in the wilderness by Moses and his brother and sister (v. 4)? And how about God's turning the intentions of a king (Balak) and famous prophet (Balaam) inside out so that the hired curser became the blesser (v. 5, cf. Numbers 22–24)? And the parting of the Jordan River so that the Israelites could walk dry-shod from Shittim in Moab to Gilgal in the Promised Land (v. 5)—was that some sort of hardship on the Israelites? No indeed, Israel owed God everything; but all the Israelites were giving him was ritual sacrifice. They were not giving him their true obedience. Thus they continued to live selfishly, carrying out or overlooking practices that were clearly unjust, immoral, and irreligious (for examples, see Micah 2:2, 8–9; 3:3–4, 9–11; 5:12; 7:3, 6).

In Matthew 23:23 we read of how Jesus criticized the Pharisees for ignoring exactly what Micah's audience ignored, the need to *be* righteous and not just to follow procedures with technical precision.

Historical Setting

Micah (740–690 B.C.) witnessed the same sorts of social and economic injustices and the same sort of idolatry and general disregard for the law of God that his contemporaries Isaiah, Hosea, and Amos all spoke of. He, like they, lived among people who kept up the formal side of their religion very nicely, by sacrificing—the main act of worship—faithfully. But these same sacrificers were in fact hypocrites, because while carefully obeying the law's requirements for sacrifice (Leviticus 1–5) they ignored the law's demand for right living (Leviticus 19:18; etc.).

The misuse and abuse of innocent people for personal profit and power was widespread. The Israelites had forgotten their God and what he had done for them (Micah 6:3–5). They did not need either more sacrifices or more intense sacrificing (vs. 6–7). What they needed was to walk with God.

Form and Structure

This poetic passage follows a format known as the Covenant Lawsuit. People in ancient Israel saw court cases regularly, as they passed through the city gates where court was held (e.g., Ruth 4:1–9). Borrowing on this familiarity, the prophets often portrayed the Lord and Israel as opponents in a court case. The Lord was usually the prosecutor, often the plaintiff, and always the judge. Israel was the defendant, against whom the evidence was presented.

That is what's happening here in Micah 6:1–8. The questions to Israel are the questions of prosecutor or plaintiff, and the challenge of verse 8 is a challenge to keep the law revealed to Israel on Mt. Sinai, a law calling for a fair, decent, compassionate, generous, and obedient life-style.

The command to "walk humbly with your God" that concludes the passage has sometimes been misunderstood. The passage is not talking about good attitudes but about right practices. Thus the meaning of the last statement can hardly be "think of yourself meekly" or the like. Rather, it means that we should not walk (a common term for "live") selfishly, inconsiderately, or improperly. Thus the translation "walk properly with your God," while less memorable, might help clarify the intent of the wording here.

Application

1. Faithful participation in worship is not enough. It must be accompanied by faithful, proper living.
2. A good look at the past reminds us of God's loyalty, and of our responsibility to be loyal to him in return.